SAMUEL BECKETT

A BEGINNER'S GUIDE

STEVE COOTS

Series Editors
Rob Abbott & Charlie Bell

Hodder & Stoughton

A MEMBER OF THE HODDER HEADLINE GROUP

Orders: please contact Bookpoint Ltd, 130 Milton Park, Abingdon, Oxon OX14 4SB. Telephone: (44) 01235 400414, Fax: (44) 01235 400454. Lines are open from 9.00–6.00, Monday to Saturday, with a 24-hour message answering service. Email address: orders@bookpoint.co.uk

British Library Cataloguing in Publication Data
A catalogue record for this title is available from The British Library

ISBN 0 340 80273 1

First published 2001
Impression number   10 9 8 7 6 5 4 3 2 1
Year   2005 2004 2003 2002 2001

Typeset by Transet Limited, Coventry, England.
Printed in Great Britain for Hodder & Stoughton Educational, a division of Hodder Headline Plc, 338 Euston Road, London NW1 3BH by Cox & Wyman, Reading, Berks

CONTENTS

How To Use This Book

The *Beginner's Guide* series aims to introduce readers to the major writers of the past 500 years. It is assumed that readers will begin with little or no knowledge and will want to go on to explore Beckett in other ways.

BEGIN BY READING THE AUTHOR

This book is a companion guide to Beckett's major works: it is not a substitute for reading the works themselves or, even better, seeing Beckett performed on stage. This will help you put theory into practice. The book is divided into sections. After considering how to approach the author's work and a brief biography, we go on to explore some of the main writings and themes before examining some critical approaches. The survey finishes with suggestions for further reading and possible areas of further study.

HOW TO APPROACH UNFAMILIAR OR DIFFICULT TEXTS

Coming across a new writer can seem daunting, but do not be put off. The trick is to persevere. Much good writing is multi-layered and complex. It is precisely this diversity and complexity which makes literature rewarding and exhilarating.

Literature often needs to be read more than once, and in different ways. These ways can include: a leisurely and superficial reading to get the main ideas and narrative; a slower more detailed reading focusing on the nuances of the text, concentrating on what appear to be key passages; and reading in a random way, moving back and forth through the text to examine such things as themes, or narrative or characterization. Each reader has their own approach but undoubtedly the best way to extract the most from a text is to read it several times.

In complex texts it may be necessary to read in short chunks. Sometimes the only way to get by is to skip through the text, going back over it later. When it comes to tackling difficult words or concepts it is often enough to guess in context on the first reading, making a more detailed study using a dictionary or book of critical concepts on later reading. If you prefer to look up unusual words as you go along, be careful that you do not disrupt the flow of the text and your concentration.

USING BIOGRAPHICAL MATERIAL

Opinions differ about whether it is useful to know something of a writer's life and times before reading a text. It can certainly be fascinating to know something about an author. The information gleaned can be illuminating but it can also be irrelevant and misleading and should be treated with caution. It might be that the author wishes us to engage primarily with the text itself, which is usually offered to the public with little meaningful biographical content. It should be possible with most authors to enjoy their work without knowing anything about them. Indeed, one strand of modern literary criticism argues that the author is entirely irrelevant to a text.

VOCABULARY

You will see that KEY TERMS and unfamiliar words are set in **bold** text. These words are defined and explained in the GLOSSARY to be found at the back of the book. In order to help you further we have also summarized each section in our SUMMARY sections.

You can read this introductory guide in its entirety, or dip in wherever suits you. You can read it in any order. It is a tool to help you appreciate a key figure in literature. We hope you enjoy reading it and find it useful.

✳ ✳ ✳ ✳*SUMMARY* ✳ ✳ ✳ ✳

To maximize the use of this book:

– read the author's work.

– read it several times in different ways.

– be open to innovative or unusual forms of writing.

– persevere.

– treat biographical information with care and deal mainly with the texts themselves.

Rob Abbott and Charlie Bell

Why read Samuel Beckett today?

THE ROAD TO SALVATION?

Nell: [*Without lowering her voice.*] Nothing is funnier than unhappiness, I grant you that. But –

Nagg: [*Shocked.*] Oh!

Nell: Yes, yes, it's the most comical thing in the world. And we laugh, we laugh, with a will, in the beginning. But it's always the same thing. Yes, it's like the funny story we have heard too often, we still find it funny but we don't laugh any more. [*Pause.*] Have you anything else to say to me?

Nagg: No.

Endgame, Faber and Faber (1986), p. 101

This section from *Endgame* holds the essence of Samuel Beckett. It is sparse, bleak and pared down to the minimum. It is pessimistic yet suggests an optimism; if you recognize your misery, then you are on the road to salvation. So why read him today?

TWENTIETH CENTURY

Beckett can be classed as a true twentieth-century writer. Not only for his commentary on the human condition during the turbulence of the period but also because his life spanned the century. Beckett was born in Ireland in 1906 and died in France in 1989.

PUSHING LANGUAGE TO THE LIMITS

Regarded as one of the last of the great **Modernists** (and possibly one of the first of the **Postmodernists**), he took the experiments and the vision of art in the first half of the

KEY TERMS

Modernism: Art movement of the late nineteenth and early twentieth centuries. The movement challenged established artistic conventions and celebrated new technologies and thought.

Postmodernism: Art movement of the late twentieth century. Grew out of Modernism. Concentrated on *how* the artist sees rather than *what* the artist sees. The movement encouraged mixing genres, fragmenting forms and exploring the issues of nature, status and role.

Beckett covered the twentieth century

twentieth century to a new manifestation in the latter half. He explored the forms of literature and took a radical approach to the theatre. He pared his language and his characters down to practically nothing to try and get to the true identity and essence of what it is to be human.

RELEVANCE

The resonance of Beckett's svelte body of work echoes about us today. The uncertainty of why we are here, the ultimate futility of our actions and the absurdity of life in general are very much our contemporary concerns. The rise of therapy in the 1980s, the plethora of television programmes like *Oprah* or *Montel Williams* exploring the way we live, or the explosion of 'lifestyle' magazines demonstrates this. Beckett is as pertinent as ever with his questioning outlook and explorations of our state of being.

AHEAD OF HIS TIME

His collected work is not vast. The novel trilogy (*Molloy*, *Malone Dies* and *The Unnamable*) and four full-length plays formed the major part of his output. Beckett, instead, concentrated on fragments, short stories and, what he termed, 'dramaticules' – short theatrical pieces like *Rockaby* which was only 15 minutes long.

As well as the work for the stage he wrote for television and radio. He experimented with using music as part of the dialogue structure (*Cascando*), with the choreography of his actors to create a dramatic, physical dialogue (*Quad*) and even used the stage itself as a character (*Breath*). His work can be seen as a forerunner to and exponent of the **performance art** that we have today such as in the work of Joseph Beuys, Gilbert and George and even to the winner of the Turner Prize in 1999, Steve McQueen with his video variation on a stunt by Buster Keaton.

KEY TERM

Performance art: A form of artistic expression that uses live performance, installations, film and video. An artwork that is performed in a live or recorded form. Although culled from theatrical theory, its concerns are that of the artist as opposed to dramatist.

AN EXPERIMENTER

An example of how his experimentation existed independently of creative traditions is a rare piece made in 1966. Beckett took his play *Play* (*Comedie* in the original French) and, with the film-maker Martin Karmitz, turned it into an 18-minute film. Rather than just make a copy of the theatre production, Beckett utilized, for the time, quite radical film techniques such as rapid cutting, slow pans, extreme lighting and a speeded-up soundtrack to emphasize the pace of the dialogue. The soundtrack was then manipulated tone-wise to maintain the correct vocal sound.

It never made it to the cinema and lay redundant for many years. Now, at the turn of the twentieth century it has found a home in art galleries. The Anthony Reynolds Gallery, London showed it as a piece of video art in 2001.

NEW MEDIA

The concept of **video art** was not to emerge until, roughly, the 1970s. The film of *Play* is a prime example of how Beckett embraced whatever medium he chose and experimented with it. It also demonstrates that he had no concerns about maintaining convention. His prime motivation with the realization of his work was to get as close to what he had in his mind as possible. The critic Adrian Searle in his review of the filmed *Play* (*Guardian*, 9 December 2000) says:

> The film's technique may have been superseded, yet shown in a gallery, *Comedie* could almost be a film installation by any number of contemporary artists. Except of course it is better, more radical, more extreme than most.

If Beckett were alive today, he would have embraced this new media of film, video and computer imaging. As it was, back in the 1940s, when he was making a name for himself, the theatre was the only medium that could come halfway to sustaining his vision.

BECKETT'S CONTINUED INFLUENCE

Beckett's minimal approach to his work and his radical freeing of the traditions of writing and theatre has influenced and informed many of the artists working today. The playwrights Harold Pinter and Tom Stoppard bear his influence; the composers Steve Reich and Philip Glass carry echoes of Beckett's sparsity and repeated phrasing; and the word 'Beckettian' has entered our language as meaning bleak and doleful.

Beckett was a writer who was never afraid to go beyond the limits of his medium. He was one of the pioneers of the twentieth century who helped redefine the traditions that preceded him. His work was part of the **zeitgeist** in the changing 1950s, 1960s and 1970s that freed up artistic expression. Whether we have seen or read his work or not, his dark vision has pervaded our consciousness.

Beckett broke free from constraint

*＊＊＊SUMMARY ＊＊＊＊

● Beckett is relevant to us today because of:

– his modern preoccupation with exploring the facets of human existence.

– his willingness to experiment thus influencing current creative issues.

– his contribution to laying a foundation for the development of contemporary arts.

– his emotional connection to failure and futility.

– his shrewd appraisal of life in terms of apparent death or near death experience.

2 How to approach Beckett's work

FIRST CONTACT

On first encountering Beckett's writing the reader (or viewer) may find themselves intrigued, if a little bemused, especially with his later prose such as *Nohow On*. The words and sentences are terse to the point of obscurity. The **stream of consciousness style**, as in *The Unnamable*, can be difficult for those unprepared for it.

READ THE WORK ALOUD

The words on the page need to be read aloud if the full expression of the work is to be understood. This applies to the prose as much as it does to the plays. Beckett's work, though sparse, is very rich in musicality. Understanding his love of music helps here. His work can be treated as music made up of words rather than notes. Let the words and situations flow as you read them.

An example of this is one of his last pieces, *What is the Word* included in *Stirrings Still*. If you read this extract aloud, the musicality of the work starts to dominate over the sense:

> where-
> what is the word-
> there-
> over there-
> away over there-
> afar-
> afar away over there-
> afaint-
> afaint afar away over there what-
> what-

what is the word-
seeing all this-
all this this-
all this this here-
folly for to see what-

Stirrings Still, John Calder, (1999), p. 27

COMPREHENDING THE INCOMPREHENSIBLE

Beckett writes in a fractured way especially when dealing with the narrative or story. In his trilogy of novels scenes and fragments of narrative flit here and there, characters omit chunks of explanation and there are bizarre diversions as if the narrator has drifted off into another daydream.

If you approach the work in a conventional fashion it is easy to get lost in the text and confused. This was, of course, part of the nature of his themes – the characters' fractured thoughts and confusion with their circumstances. If you think about riding a bike whilst riding a bike, you will fall off. Reading Beckett is similar. Enjoy the work first, then take your thoughts and impressions away with you.

CHARACTERIZATION

Beckett's characters are stripped down to the bare essentials of their humanity. The surroundings he puts them in are basic to the needs of the plot. He does not waste a single word. Beckett confronts his reader with this raw situation. Subsequently, any actions they make are amplified and appear absurd. A lot of the humour of his work is drawn from our reaction to these, now ridiculous, actions. The tragedy follows when we recognize ourselves doing these self-same actions for ourselves. We have not seen them so exposed as when Beckett shows them to us.

THE PROBLEM OF MEANING

Beckett's sparseness can also be problematic: what exactly does it all mean? In one of the few statements that he made on his work he stated: 'It means exactly what I have written.'

Readers will be compelled to project their own interpretation on the work. We all have our idea on what it is to be human and Beckett reflects this in his writing. In effect he reflects *us* in his work. This is another reason to bring an open mind to the work. As the composer Philip Glass writes:

> Beckett's [work] doesn't exist separately from its relationship to the viewer, who is included as part of the play's content.
>
> P. Glass, *Einstein on the Beach*, Faber and Faber, (1988), p. 36

Beckett with an enigmatic tree

SYMBOLISM

Because there is very little happening on stage (or in the text), everything becomes significant and pregnant with potential meaning. If we take the tree in *Godot* for instance it could symbolize:

* the tree of life (as in the Kabbala or in biblical terms)
* the tree of good and evil
* Dante's tree at the gates of hell

* the pine tree in Japanese Noh plays
* the Norse mythological tree Yggdrasil
* the Buddhist Bo tree
* the crucifixion cross
* a question mark
* the point of life and death
* a tree.

The choice is yours. Because Beckett never elucidated beyond what he presented, interpretation is fraught with danger and revelation. As Beckett says at the end of his novel *Watt*: 'No symbols where none intended.' It is up to the reader to determine how vague Beckett is being here, if he is being vague at all.

THE FREEDOM TO INTERPRET

This attitude may leave the audience high and dry. But it also gives a huge emotional freedom to Beckett's work. It can be known without being understood. In conversation with the playwright Harold Pinter, Beckett said:

> I was in hospital once. There was a man in another ward, dying of throat cancer. In the silence, I could hear his screams continually. That's the only kind of form my work has.
>
> J. Law *et al.* (eds), *Companion to Theatre*, Cassell (1997), p. 46

Beckett does not state that this is *why* the world is, instead he offers the reader a mirror of their own world if they are willing to see it. In this way the work is as timeless as we are.

✳ ✳ ✳ ✳ *SUMMARY* ✳ ✳ ✳ ✳

* Beckett's prose and drama should be read out loud.

* React to it emotionally rather than intellectually.

* Listen to Beckett's work as if it were music.

* Be careful of assumptions or over-interpretation. The symbolism in Beckett's work can be treacherous.

3 Biography

BEGINNINGS

Samuel Beckett was born into an affluent Anglo-Irish Protestant family in Foxrock, a prosperous suburb of Dublin. Although his actual date of birth is uncertain, the accepted and, in terms of Beckett, quite poetic date was Good Friday, 13 April 1906.

His father, William, was a quantity surveyor. When William fell ill with pneumonia, Maria (May) Roe nursed him in hospital. Their romance was swift and they married on the 31 August 1901. William (Bill as he was known in family circles) and May were opposite characters. He was an ebullient character happy with pleasure-seeking, while she was moody, possibly depressive and somewhat caustic.

Beckett had a brother, Frank, who was older than him by four years. Whereas Frank had been quite a happy baby, Samuel was a sickly child who was ill at ease, crying most of the time. It could be said that Frank was his father's child and Samuel was his mother's in temperament and appearance. His mother was a gaunt figure as was Samuel – tall and lithe with chiselled features. As an adult, Samuel cut a distinctive, lolloping figure.

EDUCATION

Beckett attended Earlsfort House School in Dublin, Portora Royal School in Enniskillen and Trinity College in Dublin where he majored in French and Italian.

At this point in time Beckett had no literary ambitions (if he had ambitions at all). He was on course for an academic teaching career and completed his Bachelor of Arts degree in 1927 and his Master of Arts in 1931.

SPORT

As well as being an excellent scholar he was a very proficient sports-
man, excelling at cricket. He was the only Nobel Prize-winning author
to be mentioned in Wisden's Cricketing Almanac, the cricketers' bible,
playing first-class cricket for Trinity against Northampton.

Sport was a major interest for him all his life. As well as the cricket he
was a capable tennis player and a combative chess player. He would
follow sport on television and radio and would always enquire about
sporting events from his visiting friends.

THE FIRST ENCOUNTER WITH FRANCE

Between 1928 and 1930 he lectured at the Ecole Normale Supérieure in
Paris as part of an exchange programme. He took over the post from
Thomas MacGreevy and the two became good friends. MacGreevy was
involved with a circle of literary friends in Paris. He soon introduced
Beckett to this circle, a circle that happened to revolve around the Irish
writer James Joyce.

FIRST WRITINGS

Beckett and Joyce became good friends and Beckett soon started to
drift from his academic lecturing towards literature. He wrote his first
pieces of prose and poetry at this time. He also wrote essays and critical articles, notably on the writer Marcel Proust as well as Joyce himself. His poem *Whoroscope* won a literary prize offered by the Hours
Press (run by Nancy Cunard) in 1930 and he started to achieve a small
success for his efforts at writing.

He returned to Dublin in 1931 to take up his teaching job at Trinity but
within four terms he resigned his post. Teaching was a profession that
he could not bear. He complained to his friends about the staff,
students and the college. Thereafter he spent time wandering through
London, Germany and France. He wrote his first novel at this time, *Fair
to Middling Women*. This was an autobiographical piece, sometimes
quite cruel about the thinly disguised characters, especially of his
sometime girlfriend Peggy Sinclair. He did not have a lot of success in

getting it published and a large part was recycled as a collection of short stories, *More Pricks than Kicks*, in 1934.

PSYCHOANALYSIS

In 1932 his father died of an unexpected heart attack. Beckett, depressed, somewhat adrift and suffering from insomnia and various psychosomatic ailments, went into two years of psychoanalysis in London. From this period of therapy he became fascinated by the theories of **Carl Gustav Jung**, especially by one of Jung's cases where it was proposed that a patient had not been fully born. This idea fascinated Beckett and proved to be a cornerstone in much of his mature writing.

> **KEY PERSON**
>
> Carl Gustav Jung: 1875–1961 psychologist. Criticized Sigmund Freud's interpretations and developed analytical psychology. Developed the concept of the collective unconscious and its archetypes.

It was during this time in London between 1934 and 1936 that he wrote his novel, *Murphy*, about an Irishman in London trying to extricate himself from the world. It was a transitional novel. Although still using autobiographical elements, the novel started to explore the darker side of Beckett's characters. From this point his writing started to gain the maturity of a growing creative mind.

THE WANDERING BOHEMIAN

Beckett continued to wander through Europe, stopping for most of the time in Paris where he became fully absorbed into the James Joyce circle. His friendship with Joyce was confidentially close, reading to Joyce as the latter's eyesight failed and working on translations into French of Joyce's work, primarily *Finnegans Wake*. This, naturally, had an influence upon his own writing. Beckett was drawing on ideas and concepts from philosophy, art, music, theatre as well as literature. He also turned to the work of **Alighieri Dante**, a favourite from childhood.

> **KEY PERSON**
>
> Alighieri Dante 1265–1321 Italian poet whose most famous work is *The Divine Comedies*. This is divided into three sections, Paradise, Inferno and Hell. Dante is guided around the regions of Hell and purgatory by the poet Virgil. In Paradise the poet's guide is the beautiful Beatrice.

THEATRE
LITERATURE
ART
OUTER SHADOW
UNOBTAINABLE SELF
HOW IT SHOULD BE

PERFORMANCE
RADIO
TV
FiLM
INNER SHADOW
UNOBTAINABLE NON-SELF
HOW IT IS

Influences in and out

Beckett travelled fairly regularly at this time, floating between Dublin, London and Europe. In 1936 he had a major falling out with his mother and left Ireland permanently. The two of them, perhaps because of their similarities, were constantly fractious with each other. Also, Beckett was following a more bohemian lifestyle at odds with the middle-class world in which his mother indulged. His shabby appearance at this time was a shock and an insult to her.

NEAR DEATH AND LIFE

In 1937 Beckett settled in Paris. He made his home in Montparnasse, a working-class area on the left bank of the Seine noted for its artistic community.

On 6 January 1938, Beckett was walking home after seeing a film with some friends. A young man approached him and after a terse conversation drew a knife and stabbed Beckett in the chest. The wound was near fatal. This incident would haunt Beckett's imagination and his writing through his whole career.

Whilst recovering in hospital he was visited by a friend (and tennis partner from 1929) Suzanne Deschevaux-Dumesnil. The two of them drew close to each other and, subsequently, were to be companions for the rest of their lives. The two married in Folkestone, England in 1961. She would be his major promoter, securing important connections that brought his work to the attention of the general public.

Beckett was later to confront his assailant who had been arrested at the time of the incident. When the case was being dealt with by the courts Beckett asked the man why he had attacked him. The man replied:

> I do not know why, sir. I'm sorry
>
> J. Knowelson, *Damned to Fame*, Bloomsbury, (1997), p. 238

This was quite a profound statement for Beckett and drew him to the idea of the complete randomness and absurdity of life.

THE SECOND WORLD WAR

At the outbreak of the Second World War in 1939, Beckett and Suzanne were settled in a flat on the Rue de Favorites in Montparnesse. At first life was not too difficult under German occupation. Beckett, although not a political animal, was not unaware of the actions of the Nazis. He soon became involved with the French Resistance and he worked as a messenger for the 'Gloria' cell. He handled and translated from French to English the flow of information about German activities. In 1942, the cell had been infiltrated and he and Suzanne made their escape to Free France (in the south of the country) moments before the Gestapo broke into their flat.

They journeyed to Roussillon in the unoccupied south of France where they spent the rest of the war years. Beckett worked as a farm labourer as well as still being partially active in the Resistance. During this time he wrote his next novel, *Watt*.

In 1944 he returned briefly to Dublin. Here he seemed to have had an artistic revelation, a sudden moment of lucidity about his writing, as if his ideas had all suddenly fallen into place.

Being an alien in France, he found it difficult to get back to Paris. To get around this he secured work with the Irish Red Cross as a storeman in St Lô. After the war he was awarded the Croix de Guerre for his war work.

AN OUTPOURING OF WRITING

From the end of the war to the early 1950s he entered his most prolific writing period. During this time he produced the main bulk of work that his reputation rests upon – *Molloy* and *Malone Dies* between 1947 and 1948; *Waiting for Godot* was written between October 1948 and January 1949; *The Unnamable* was written in 1949 and *Texts for Nothing* in 1950.

After the death of his mother in 1950, using the money bequeathed to him, Beckett purchased a retreat in Ussy-sur-Marne, 30 miles outside Paris where he did the majority of his writing.

It was during this burst of writing that he wrote solely in French. Up to then he had composed in English, but found that he was getting lost in the florid quality of the language. He turned to French as a means of discipline and focus for his ideas and style. Another reason for this was his total immersion in the language; Suzanne spoke little English and the people around him rarely spoke anything other than French. Added to this was his experience in the French Resistance where he had to be exact with his language to get across the information as economically as possible. He would abandon swathes of description in favour of a more direct approach with his words. Then in 1954 Beckett's brother, Frank, died of lung cancer.

SUCCESS

From the late 1950s Beckett quickly gained his reputation as a writer and dramatist. His work was being published and performed in Europe and America, and he was developing his skills as a director.

In 1969 Beckett was awarded the Nobel Prize for Literature. As was his wont, he did not attend the ceremony, preferring to holiday in North Africa. He reportedly gave away the prize money anonymously to his needy artist friends.

To the outside world he presented a dour figure – serious and bleakly involved with his art. His ingrained gloom seemed to instruct every line of his face. Suzanne represented him at theatre openings and social events outside of his cloistered universe. He never granted interviews other than informal chats at a local café and never discussed his work or its meaning. He frequented rehearsals for his plays but never attended with an audience during the run of the play. He disliked large public gatherings and his distinct face was forever drawn in a scowl outside of his circle of friends.

Although he was a pessimist and brooded on the darker elements of life, it was always accompanied with a twinkle in his blue eyes. His was never a terminal pessimism; suicide never played a part of his life. He endured life and survived its nonsense.

A COMPANIONABLE MAN
In his private life Beckett was a constant figure in the Paris cafés. He enjoyed the company of his artist friends and he enjoyed his drink. He shunned the media, very rarely commented on his own work and thought that his life was, in his own words, 'devoid of interest' for any biographer. To his circle of friends in Paris he was a genial and humane member of the café society, making good friends with the artistic community whether they were well known, as in the case of Joyce, the sculptor Alberto Giacometti, or struggling and unknown artists.

LAYERS OF INFLUENCE
On first coming into contact with Beckett his reputation rests in the theatre and his work was born out of the literary tradition. This being said, his plays are not just swathes of profound words. He drew a huge influence from other arts.

Literature
Beckett's most obvious influence comes from the literary world and the world of his studies at Trinity. He loved the work of Dante, returning to his treasured copy of *The Comedies* many times. Proust was another major influence and Beckett wrote an acclaimed essay on the writer published in 1931.

James Joyce's influence is clearly apparent in Beckett's early work. In effect, Beckett took up the flame after the death of Joyce in 1941, forging the bridge between Modernism and Postmodernism.

Although he never actively sought out contemporary artists, writers and theatre practitioners beyond those he called friends, he still used contemporary references in his work. For instance the resonance of the opening of *Under Milk Wood* by Dylan Thomas can be found in *What Where*.

Art

Beckett loved art. He was a constant visitor to the galleries of Europe and enjoyed the company of artists. The work of Rembrandt and the Dutch school of painting heavily influenced the look of his productions in the theatre. He was absorbed by the quality of light they used in their art and this can be seen by his exact instructions for lighting in his plays. In effect, his was creating a performance tableau based on the impression these paintings left on him. Looking at this, we can see that Beckett was very much a visual artist using the performance space as his canvas.

The painting *Arrangement in Grey and White* (Whistler's Mother) by Whistler was an influence for his play *Rockaby* written in 1980. Poussin's painting *The Deposition of Christ* was an influence on the shadowed figure giving gestures of 'helpless compassion' in *Not I*. Bellini's painting of the Madonna was an influence for *Footfalls*. Caspar David's painting *Two Men Contemplating the Moon* is almost a blueprint for the setting of *Godot*.

Music

Beckett was also a lover of music. He was a more than competent musician and enjoyed playing the work of Schubert, Chopin and Beethoven on piano. Beyond the sense of his words, the language he used in his work had a musical quality to it. They became sounds conveying emotions. The sounds, in some cases, being more potent than the sense.

Although Beckett never used music in his theatre in the traditional way of adding background textures or songs, he made constant reference to it. He composed music with the spoken word and he used music as a theatrical character. In the piece *Words and Music* (written in the early 1960s, his cousin writing the music for the BBC production) the music was part of the cast list. In *Nacht und Traume* he used the last seven bars of Schubert's music as an integral element of the piece. Another Schubert piece, *Winterreise*, about a young man's journey from a broken heart, informed much of the yearning Beckett put into his characters.

Theatre

Beckett enjoyed going to the theatre. Paris in the early part of the twentieth century, was a hotbed of innovation for the stage. He was a fan of musical and slapstick comedy. These elements are peppered throughout his work, most overtly in *Godot*.

Beckett did love the music hall. He was a great admirer of clowns and the music-hall comedians. The notion of the clown fascinated him; the way they turned failure into a heroic success. He was engaged by the art of the imperfect and the ridiculous. With *Godot*, Didi and Gogo are two clowns bathed in pathos and given a sharp edge that makes their gags and pratfalls acquire a dark potency.

Film

Beckett was very fond of the cinema. He admired the clowns of the silent screen such as Buster Keaton and Laurel and Hardy. This is evident in the way he choreographed Vladimir and Estragon in *Godot*, Hamm and Clov in *Endgame* and used visual slapstick throughout his work – the banana skin incident in *Krapp's Last Tape* for instance. The hat routine in *Godot* was influenced by the Marx Brothers routine in *Duck Soup* (1933).

END OF A LIFE

Although his relationship with Suzanne was not an overtly loving one and towards the end they lived almost separate lives, theirs was a true companionship, neither being too far from the other. They were almost two parts of the same person; hers was the more public side, his was the private and the absorbed. Suzanne died on 17 July 1989 aged 89 and Beckett died on 22 December of that year aged 83. They are buried together in Montparnasse Cemetary.

Beckett steered clear of crowds

✳ ✳ ✳ ✳ SUMMARY ✳ ✳ ✳ ✳

- Although Beckett was born in Ireland he spent most of his life in France.

- Beckett refused an academic career in teaching choosing instead a bohemian lifestyle.

- Beckett indulged his love of painting, music and sport as much as he did literature and theatre.

- He was honoured for his work with the French Resistance.

- He shunned any form of publicity, preferring his close circle of friends.

- Despite outward appearances he was an affable man.

4 Major works (1): The plays

WAITING FOR GODOT

Dislocation

We are now entering a strange, dislocated world. What *Waiting for Godot* and *Endgame* present to us is nothing more than ourselves. Yet they are so stripped of our communal security that they, at first, seem alien. It appears that we need to use assumptions or guesswork to make sense of the nonsensical. When these assumptions are stripped away what do we latch on to; nothing but ourselves?

In his essay on Beckett, Alain Robbe-Grillet explains:

> The human condition, Heidegger says, is to be there. Probably it is the theatre, more than any other mode of representing reality, which reproduces this situation most naturally. The dramatic character is on stage, that is his primary quality: he is there.

> A. Robbe-Grillet, *For a New Novel: Essays on Fiction*, Ayer Company (1965), p. 111

Samuel Beckett's encounter with this requirement afforded *a priori*, an exceptional interest: at last we would see Beckett's man, we would see Man.

Beckett's technique is to seduce the viewer and, like Virgil in Dante's *Divine Comedy*, lead them below the circles of their own humanity. Art and the surface of art become negated, absurd and pointless.

So, what is the point?

Waiting for Godot is very simple in its premise. Two characters, Estragon and Vladimir, are waiting for someone. That someone does not turn up. They carry on waiting. So, you may ask, what is the point of that? How many times have you waited for no explainable reason? Have you ever waited for a telephone call or visitor? Have you ever waited for your horse to come in or for your lottery ticket to turn into riches? We all wait. If not for God then for something of God's equal.

Knowing by not knowing

With *Waiting for Godot* we are presented with the two shabby, down-at-heel characters of Estragon and Vladimir. Although they are not defined as tramps in the text, we make a natural interpretation that they are since they are stripped bare of any form of security and social standing. But they still possess their bowler hats – a sign of a certain class at the time of writing, which gives a clue to their past.

They have moments of lucid dialogue showing that they are far from uneducated. They give clues to a respectable past. They are, though, stripped of possessions; we do not know if Gogo or Didi (their nicknames in the play) own houses or have jobs or have any kind of social standing anymore. By cryptic statements we know they have lost a lot, hinted at by the Eiffel Tower reference in Act 1:

Vladimir: [*Gloomily.*] It's all too much for one man. [*Pause. Cheerfully.*] On the other hand what's the good of losing heart now, that's what I say. We should have thought of it a million years ago, in the nineties.

Estragon: Ah stop blathering and help me off with this bloody thing.

Vladimir: Hand in hand from the top of the Eiffel Tower, among the first. We were presentable in those days. Now it's too late. They wouldn't even let us up. [*Estragon tears at his boot.*] What are you doing?

Waiting for Godot, Faber and Faber (1986), p. 12

Contemporary allusions

Waiting for Godot was written in a time when Europe was scabby with the aftermath of the Second World War. There were many displaced people. Houses were ruinous and possessions were ripped away. Nothing was certain except for a *belief* of some kind that somehow kept people together against all odds. Beckett saw this and exploited it to get to grips with what it was to be a human being. He opened this wound and exposed it for what it was. Out of this *Waiting for Godot* was born.

Godot as metaphor

Some critics felt that Godot was a metaphor for God. This was an interpretation of simplistic wordplay. Although Beckett was raised in a fairly strict Protestant environment he remained, more or less, an atheist in his writing. Godot was a fairly common surname in France; indeed, there was a noted cyclist in the Tour de France called Godot at the time of writing the play and a character in Balzac's play, *Le Faiseur* (also known as *Mercadet*), is named Godeau. Beckett, though, was not unaware of this connection with the Almighty and used the name knowing of the connection.

In an example from Act 1 we can see Beckett take a potshot at religion. Didi is trying to tell Gogo the story of the two thieves crucified with Jesus. He is trying to explain that only one of the four Evangelists who witnessed the scene commented that one of the thieves was saved.

Vladimir: But one of the four says that one of the two was saved.
Estragon: Well? They don't agree, and that's all there is to it.
Vladimir: But all four were there. And only one speaks of a thief being saved. Why believe him rather than the others?
Estragon: Who believes him?
Vladimir: Everybody. It's the only version they know.
Estragon: People are bloody ignorant apes.

Waiting for Godot, Faber and Faber (1986), p. 15

The genesis of *Godot*

They play itself was written very quickly between October 1948 and January 1949. He wrote it in a child's exercise book, starting in one direction and doubling back. It was, according to Beckett, a release from the blackness of writing the first parts of his trilogy *Molloy, Malone Dies* and (after *Waiting for Godot*) *The Unnamable. Waiting for Godot* appeared almost fully formed with only the smallest of changes taking place, mainly in the translation from French into English or German, or when put into production (see *The Theatrical Notebooks of Samuel Beckett,* Faber and Faber).

The cast

So, we have two characters waiting. Two other characters enter into the scene of the road, a tree and a mound – Lucky and Pozzo. These are two characters (a master and slave) that seem to help Gogo and Didi pass the time. A fifth character, a young boy, appears to tell Gogo and Didi that Godot cannot make the appointment but will be there tomorrow. This is a reflection of the Red Queen in *Alice through the Looking Glass* whereby she states: 'Jam tomorrow, jam yesterday, but never jam today.' Yet Didi and Gogo are willing to wait.

The enigma of waiting

It is never made clear why they are waiting or why Godot is important to them. Godot could be a landowner, their God or someone with an important message (a possible reference to the Resistance work that Beckett was involved with during the war). All that is important is that they must wait for him. The metaphor concerns waiting – anytime, anywhere.

This could have been and, in some cases was, very frustrating for the audience. Godot was 'a mystery wrapped in an enigma' according to Brooks Atkinson of the *New York Times* (1953).

Burlesque

The play was peppered with slapstick, philosophical musings and confrontations. It was outrageous with the way the characters filled the period of the performance by seemingly doing very little.

An example of their game-playing comes in Act 2 where they insult each other to pass the time.

Vladimir: Moron!
Estragon: That's the idea, let's abuse each other.
[*They turn, move apart, turn again and face each other.*]
Vladimir: Moron!
Estragon: Vermin!
Vladimir: Abortion!
Estragon: Morpion!

Vladimir:	Sewer-rat!
Estragon:	Curate!
Vladimir:	Cretin!
Estragon:	[*With finality.*] Critic!
Vladimir:	Oh!

[*He wilts, vanquished, and turns away.*]

Waiting for Godot, Faber and Faber (1986), p. 70

This is also a good example for illustrating Beckett's craft with words – the way the sounds flow from one insult to the other – and his humour with a swipe at curates and critics.

Drama-less drama

The play is not chock-a-block with action but it is profound in its dealings with its themes – who we are and why we are. The play does not necessarily demand deep, analytical thought (yet many have tried to subject it to this process, which is, perhaps, what literary criticism is all about?) but it does leave an afterglow of a deeply absorbing nature. Although Godot does not turn up (sorry to spoil the ending), that is probably the most disturbing thing to happen and it is difficult to explain.

Moving away from realism

Up until this point of the 1950s, popular theatre had been very **naturalistic**. Writers like Noel Coward, George Bernard Shaw and Christopher Fry had their fingerprints all over the floorboards. Theatre represented the real world. That is, it presented to the audience a pastiche of the world as a direct copy of the drawing rooms the audience lived in.

Beckett disposed of this. His theatre was a natural progression of his prose work and, especially, with the advent of the **Theatre of the Absurd** with writers like Pirandello,

KEY TERMS

Naturalistic: Art that is a true representation or copy of the world. The world is recreated on stage or in writing or paint.

Theatre of the Absurd: A theatrical type whereby the normal conventions of theatre are ignored or modified to present life as irrational or meaning-less.

Artaud, Jarré and Ionesco. He found a freedom in the experimental theatre. Beckett, though, was the first to put across this kind of avant-garde theatre in a way that was accessible to a wider audience. *Waiting for Godot*, although not completely understood, was not rejected. This was a major step for the ideas that Beckett promoted and shared with the avant-garde of Paris at the time. He wanted to explore the situation of the human condition. Beckett became popular without losing his credibility of the avant garde.

ENDGAME

Master and slave

Endgame followed *Waiting for Godot* by six years. Like *Waiting for Godot*, *Endgame* had two main protagonists, Hamm and Clov. Hamm was the master, crippled in his mobile chair. Clov was his slave, at Hamm's beck and call. In a way, Hamm and Clov could be seen as a

Beckett plays with the narrative

progression of Pozzo and Lucky or even Didi and Gogo. Clov wheels Hamm about. As the title suggests, this is a futile exercise akin to moving the king to avoid checkmate in a lost game of chess.

The internal landscape

Whereas *Waiting for Godot* was set on a roadside, *Endgame* was very much an interior piece. It can be postulated that the scenario is the inside of a skull, or at a point between life and death. Beckett was very astute at leaving decisions to the viewer, and at the same time leaving the critic somewhat high and dry.

Either way, Hamm and Clov are seemingly trapped, not only in the environment but also in their relationship with each other. Neither can exist without the other. There are two other characters, Nagg and Nell. They are referred to as the parents of Hamm and reside in dustbins. They make only an occasional appearance, much to the annoyance of Hamm. Yet they have a resonance in the whole piece. Without being obvious, they act as parental guilt on Hamm. This he passes down to Clov. But Clov is almost in cahoots with the parents, pandering to Hamm's desperate need to control and letting him believe in this illusion of power even though this is the least of his abilities.

Hamm: Silence!
[*Nagg starts, cuts short his laugh.*]
Nell: You could see down to the bottom.
Hamm: [*Exasperated.*] Have you not finished? Will you never finish? [*With sudden fury.*] Will this never finish? [*Nagg disappears into his bin, closes the lid behind him. Nell does not move.*] [*Frenziedly.*] My kingdom for a nightman! [*He whistles. Enter Clov.*]   Clear away this muck! Chuck it into the sea! [*Clov goes to the bins, halts.*]
Nell: So white.
Hamm: What? What is she blathering about?
[*Clov stoops, takes Nell's hand, feels her pulse*]
Nell: [*To Clov.*] Desert!
[*Clov lets go her hand, pushes her back in the bin, closes the lid.*]
Clov: [*Returning to his place beside the chair.*] She has no pulse.

Hamm:	What was she drivelling about?
Clov:	She told me to go away, into the desert.
Hamm:	Damn busybody! Is that all?

Endgame, Faber and Faber (1986), p. 103

Survival

This play, like *Waiting for Godot*, has an eternal, if not interminable, feel about it. It is bleak and caustic – especially the relationship between the two main protagonists. The ending is not an end to their situation, only a terrible extenuation of their eternal misery. The play ends in stalemate.

In both *Godot* and *Endgame*, the characters somehow survive. They never crumble or give in. Didi and Gogo never abandon their mission. Hamm and Clov never tire of playing their roles. Humanity, at its most defeated, survives against all odds – this, of course being the state of Europe after the war when Beckett composed these pieces. The paradox of Beckett is that, despite being a well-documented pessimist, he is the grandest optimist of all.

THE HUMOUR IN THE PLAYS

Waiting for Godot is a very funny play, especially if it is played according to Beckett's direction. It employs slapstick, wordplay and farcical situations – all well used and commonplace devices. There are overtones of Laurel and Hardy or Abbott and Costello in the character's interaction. *Endgame* is funny as well, but in a much blacker fashion. Both play on the music-hall fashion of quick banter and comic timing. It was actually suggested that Laurel and Hardy would be ideal to play Gogo and Didi. Regardless of this intriguing suggestion, many comedians have played the roles to some success. Yet comedians in these 'serious' dramatic roles have left the audience perplexed.

The hat-swapping scene from *Godot* is a good example of the slapstick Beckett employed.

[*Estragon takes Vladimir's hat. Vladimir adjusts Lucky's hat on his head. Estragon puts on Vladimir's hat in place of his own which he hands to Vladimir. Vladimir takes Estragon's hat. Estragon adjusts Vladimir's hat on his head. Vladimir puts on Estragon's hat in place of Lucky's which he hands to Estragon. Estragon takes Lucky's hat. Vladimir adjusts Estragon's hat on his head. And so on until: Estragon takes Vladimir's hat. Vladimir adjusts Lucky's hat on his head. Estragon hands Vladimir's hat back to Vladimir who takes it and hands it back to Estragon who takes it and hands it back to Vladimir who takes it and throws it down.*]

Waiting for Godot, Faber and Faber (1986), p. 67

Those wanting out-and-out hysterics have been pulled up short. Those wanting brow-knitting seriousness have been left bemused. Beckett has had to forge his own, unique artistic path . This has been an enduring problem with his work; it falls between the camps of the highbrow and the popular and neither camp has been willing to bridge the gap. Beckett sat outside of everything it seems; not mad enough for the theatre's anarchists, not sane enough for the conventional. There were not enough jokes for a comedy but many too many for a true tragedy. He sat at his own café table surrounded by the houses of artistic genres, never aligning himself with any of them.

DARKNESS

Both *Waiting for Godot* and *Endgame* are potent plays. They are dark in their intentions and no amount of analysis can fully unravel their mystery. But they work in their strange ways, leaving the viewer with an unspoken

> **KEY TERM**
>
> Dramaturgy: The study and practice of theatre and drama.

feeling of understanding. They freed up the theatre, both at their time of writing and in today's **dramaturgy**. Even now there is still a certain amount of dismissal of them for being bleak, pointless or dour.

INTERPRETATIONS

Beckett has put the viewer in a difficult position. Any rejection of his writing brings about an accusation of miscomprehension, yet to acknowledge their meaning begs the question of misinterpretation.

Maybe we should view them with a small smile and a glint in the eye. His landscape is ours. He did not set out to define the world, he merely presents it to us.

KRAPP'S LAST TAPE

Together with the ensemble dramas (such as *Waiting for Godot*, *Endgame* and *Happy Days*) Beckett wrote pieces for the single voice. These included monologues with only one actor on stage (*Krapp's Last Tape*) and plays where there is only one speaking part but other figures are present (*Not I*).

Krapps' last tape

An accessible piece

Compared to Beckett's other work, *Krapp's Last Tape*, is very straight-forward and accessible. Krapp, a 69-year-old man resides in his 'den' and is involved in quite a conventional occupation of recording his memoirs. The opening, where he eats a banana and casts the skin aside then slips on it has overtones of silent comedy pratfalls. The initial interaction Krapp has with his recordings are quite jovial; both Krapp and his past voice laughing along together. The play then becomes darker as Krapp explores the contents of the tape he has selected. This raises the question in the mind of the audience of why spool five was selected and thus raises the anticipation of what memory is going to be visited.

IDENTITY OVER TIME

The tapes form a diary that he has recorded annually. Although record-ed by the same person, the effect of listening back gives the illusion of two distinct people on stage. The themes of identity are thus raised – are we the same person at all when confronted by the passage of time?

Krapp is confronted by this dilemma of who is the *real* person – the one listening or the voice from the past. Krapp vocalizes his distaste for his younger self:

> Just been listening to that stupid bastard I took myself for thirty years ago, hard to believe I was as bad as that. Thank God that's all done away with.
>
> *Krapps Last Tape*, Faber and Faber (1986), p. 222

Yet he returns with yearning to that part of the tape that recounts a sex-ual encounter. Krapp treats his machine as a confidant, embracing it as a true companion.

As with much of Beckett's other work, there is an enigma within the play. Which is the 'last' tape? Is it 'spooool' five which is the last tape with which he reminisces and which ends the play? Or is it the record-ing he makes during the play, which would be his last tape?

Death

There are strong overtones of death in the work. There's reference to the physical death of his mother; he refers to the perambulator pushed by the nurse as 'funereal'. The spool is recorded in Krapp's ledger with notes that include 'Mother at rest at last' and 'Farewell to love' – a reference to the death of a relationship. The play points to the death of the spirit, memory and the self.

Yet, by the fact that Krapp's diaries are on tape, the past and Krapp's life is kept alive even beyond his eventual physical demise. This acts in a way not only to trap and torture him but also to preserve himself, his past selves and identities. The tapes keep him whole and at the same time maintain his fractured identity.

Specially written

Krapp's Last Tape was written in 1958 for a specific actor, Patrick Magee. His sonorous voice had captured Beckett's imagination after he heard him read from *Molloy* and *From an Abandoned* work on the BBC. This play was written in English and provisionally titled *Magee's Monologue*.

NOT I

Not I, written in English in 1972, has an abstract setting. All that is visible is the mouth of the speaking actor who is elevated 8 feet above the stage. The other character is across the stage and is a non speaking role, only giving small, physical gestures of 'helpless compassion'.

Identity separation

With *Krapp's Last Tape* there is an effort to give identity a physicality (if not by action, then by the conscious act of recording); *Not I* works in an opposite way. Here, the narrator is defiantly separating identities. She is recounting a story of trauma, rape and birth in an adamantly third person fashion. The aggressiveness of this act implies the only conclusion that the person she is talking about is herself.

Yet, seen in the context of a psychoanalytical reading, it is understandable. The conclusion that can easily be drawn is that of someone in total denial. She has separated herself from herself. She talks about herself as an other. To do otherwise would be too painful and ultimately destructive:

> ... sink face down in the grass ... nothing but the larks ... so on ... grabbing at the straw ... straining to hear ... the odd word ... make some

sense of it ... whole body like gone ... just the mouth ... like maddened ... and can't stop ... no sopping it ... something she- ... something she had to- ... what? ... who? ... no! ... she!

Not I, Faber and Faber (1986), p. 381

So, with this scenario, we see Beckett at his most survivalist again. Mouth is willing to share her most painful moments but in disguise. By disguising she survives. This is not doom and gloom this is celebration: Mouth is communicating.

The bare minimum

All the audience sees is the mouth, a scarlet orifice suspended above the stage and a shadowy, covered figure downstage. Again, Beckett is obscure with his intention – or all too obvious. The mouth is all we are allowed to see of the narrator. It is all we have to piece together the personality, the psyche and the presence. The Auditor, down stage, is impotent, merely listening and reacting in a passive way.

The mouth is open to interpretation – and misinterpretation. It could be an eye; it could be a vagina; it could be a wound; it could be an anus; it could be an orchid; it could be a number 9 Routemaster double-decker bus. Knowing that Beckett leaves nothing to chance, it is safe to assume that 'Mouth' is a mouth. But then, what is a 'mouth'? It is the point where nourishment is taken and communication is made.

It could be said that Mouth takes nourishment from the attentive audience. Certainly the dialogue is presented at breakneck speed, as if to get the words out as soon as possible; to get the ordeal over and done with, then to receive the repayment of acceptance from the listeners even though the piece has no defined beginning or end. A great faith is needed to tell the story. At any point there could be rejection, incredulousness and ridicule. Mouth persists, waging all against these potential reactions. Nobody has to listen but they do.

Therapy

All the way through Mouth constantly reaffirms her position that she is not the subject of the narrative, making herself anonymous within the text. We know nothing of her from herself and we see nothing of her from the auditorium. She is as anonymous as she could possibly be without losing that contact with the listener. This is a state that we would all like to achieve in times of ultimate stress.

With this play, Beckett taps into the modern mind. He almost foretold the growth of therapy and counselling in the later part of the twentieth century. The audience takes on the role of the therapist listening to the patient's heartfelt outpourings.

Mouth lays herself open in her need to communicate. In the 1970s, when this piece was written, this was a painful thing to experience. Now, it is commonplace but the writing has not lost its potency. Indeed, the themes of uncertainty in the world and sexual abuse are as relevant as they were, only more open. It would be far fetched to say that Beckett had anything to do with this openness, but he was certainly ahead of the game with the risks he took in his writing.

Purity

Both *Krapp's Last Tape* and *Not I* explore theatre. *Not I* strips the stage down to the bare minimum to present his writing in a pure fashion; writing that is regarded as possibly his finest and most poetic. *Krapp's Last Tape* shows his writing at its most obvious, yet most dense. What is gleaned from the stage is only the beginning.

Both plays are obvious and can be taken on a surface level. *Not I* is exhilarating, *Krapp's Last Tape* is slow burning. Both plays, also, leave an impression that the viewer will take away with them. Beckett works in a very **subliminal** way: his concerns slowly unravel in the mind. The material burns into the subconscious, extracting from the viewer a world that is uncomfortable. Unlike other theatre where the audience can leave the concepts contained on stage, Beckett places his stage firmly in the mind of the audience.

> **KEY TERM**
>
> Subliminal: Information absorbed by someone without them being aware of the process. For example, subliminal advertising is a means of communicating advertising to a viewer without them realizing.

5 Major works (2): The prose

MOLLOY

Written in Beckett's most prolific period between 1947 and 1953, this trilogy is probably the most profound of all of his prose writing. *Molloy* and *Malone Dies* began the period. They were written after his 'revelation' whilst watching the sea on the banks of his homeland in 1946. This revelation, told him that:

> instead of writing about that exterior world he should have written about the inner world with its darkness, ignorance, its uncertainty.

> A. Cronin, *The Last Modernist*, Flamingo (1997), p. 359

From this point Beckett took a huge departure from the conventional narrative flow and dramatization of character of the time.

Dislocated narrative

The novels form a very disconnected story line. The narrative seems to have very little grounding. Nothing seems to happen except for a seemingly disembodied voice wittering on about seemingly inconsequential events. Out of this slowly emerges narrative reality. The last line of *Molloy* gives us a clue that all may not be as it seems:

> Then I went back into the house and wrote. It is midnight. The rain is beating on the windows. It was not midnight. It was not raining.

> *Molloy*, Picador (1980), p. 162

In *Molloy* we are given the narrative in two halves. These two halves are, according to our conventional narrative understanding, back to front. But the reader only knows this at the end of the piece. Conventionally, the reader needs to have a sense of narrative to be able to recognize the flow of the writing. We are familiar with the notion that a story has a beginning, middle and end. If the reader does not have this then the piece becomes a jumble of nonsense. Beckett plays with this, pushing the reader to the limit of their comprehension. Beckett presents the reader with middle, end, middle, then beginning.

This is what Beckett probably did best. He pushed his audience to the edge of their understanding and then took them further. He did this with profound conviction, which is why his readers stayed with him and why other writers may have failed in the same pursuit. Above all else, Beckett had an unshakeable belief in his writing. Arrogance maybe, but a belief nonetheless.

Playing games

Beckett played with the notion of character. He blurred the delineation between who was narrator and who was being recounted. Could we say that Molloy was Moran? Is the insufferable character of Part Two of *Molloy* really on the decline to become the decrepit character of Molloy of whom he is searching for? The ending loops the reader back in the fashion of a white-knuckle ride. It comes as a shock to the reader.

A straightforward tale?

Molloy is probably the most straightforward book of the trilogy. There is some semblance of action. We have a pursued and a pursuer. Molloy, in the first part, has to produce reports but seems to wander off in search of his mother. He is damaged in the legs and ends up crawling through the forest. Moran, the pursuer, with his useless son in tow, is put on the case. Moran is an undescribed agent in search of Molloy. If ever we have a search for the self, this is it. Moran is in search of what he becomes.

The novel is absurd. Both Molloy and Moran are ridiculous characters. Molloy is out of control and Moran is too in control. Again, knowing that one transmutes into the other we see how fragile both states are; they infect and disease each other – one by fear, the other by specious authority.

Waffle

Molloy, though, takes a long time to get to that point. There is a lot of what seems to be insubstantial waffle to get through. This has a way of making the eventual outcome all the more potent. Surely, is that not how life is? A fictional narrative has only the relevant action to move the reader through to the **denouement**. Beckett fills his writing with the fluff and nonsense of the everyday, only giving out a glimpse, here and there, as to what is *actually* going on. Molloy's obsession with counting his sucking stones for instance, or Moran's over-bearing concern of his son's stamp collection.

KEY TERMS

Denouement: The final clarification or resolution of a narrative.

Metaphor: A figure of speech in which a word or phrase is applied to an object or action that it does not literally denote in order to imply a resemblance.

MALONE DIES

With *Malone Dies*, the reader is suddenly placed into a static, internal world. Here, the narrator is a bed-bound man seemingly at the end of his life. He knows that this is an inevitability and so fills his time with recounting stories in between accounts of how he spends his time in the room. As in *Not I* there is a feeling of denial. At first Malone's stories are disjointed accounts of inconsequential people. He tells tales of which the reader can only grow tired. That is until they start to pick up hints of the present storyteller's existence. Then the stories become autobiographical, especially when the narrative takes on the shadow of the present. Malone is fracturing his journey to his present state into dispossessed shards. As in *Not I*, this can be seen as a personal defence. This said, it is still futile and Malone revels in this, playing up to his demise by toying with and misleading the reader.

In this following example from *Malone Dies*, Malone is thinking about the nurse who tends him. He once had an affair with her yet now feels repulsed by her. This can be taken as a **metaphor** for his revolted outlook on the whole of his situation

> Inauspicious beginnings indeed, during which his feeling for Moll was frankly one of repugnance. Her lips in particular repelled him, those selfsame lips, or so little changed as to make no matter, that some months later he was to suck with grunts of pleasure, so that at the very sight of them he not only closed his eyes, but covered them with his hands for greater safety.

Malone Dies, Picador (1980), p. 241

Disguised identities

Malone Dies follows a similar pattern to *Molloy* in the way that Beckett disguises identities and confounds the narrative plot. Both play with expectations and turn those expectations back on themselves. *Malone Dies* takes the concepts of *Molloy* further. Then we have *The Unnamable* that rarefies the theme even further. The characters throughout the Trilogy become memories or figments of the narrator in this final novel. What was real becomes fiction until nothing tangible seems to be left.

THE UNNAMABLE

In *The Unnamable*, the narrator is a totally disembodied soul. He exists in a no man's land of thought. Physically, he exists in a glass jar; yet even this seems to fade until all we have are words. All the way through there are references to characters in the previous novels of Beckett. A hint is being dropped. The trilogy could be manifesting into a journey through Beckett's creative process:

> Ah if I could only find a voice of my own, in all this babble, it would be the end of their troubles, and of mine.

> *The Unnamable*, Picador (1980) p. 320

Beckett as The Unnamable

An evaporating hero

Here the words are truly filling in time. There are snippets of home-spun philosophy, a raging against circumstance and a feeling of the fear of stopping. Everything is disembodied as if a drawing is being slowly erased. Only the spoken words can pin down existence, can prove that the narrator is real. There is panic in the sentences that cast aside full-stops as if the full stop is the death knell. The words rattle on, never relenting, never letting the reader go. The information contained is almost irrelevant – the narrator has to go on.

> No need to think in order to despair. Agreed then on monotony, it's more stimulating.
>
> *The Unnamable*, Picador (1980), p. 338

Rather than using the *sense* of the writing to convey a message, Beckett is using the *effect* of writing to communicate. In the end, after the narrator has almost been erased completely comes the statement:

> I can't go on. I'll go on.
>
> *The Unnamable*, Picador (1980), p. 382

Is this the statement of relief or torture? Is it the essence of a voice with the base instinct of survival at all costs?

AN OVERVIEW

No piece of Beckett's writing is independent from any other piece. We have seen the constant references to Beckett's early work in the trilogy. The novella *Mercier and Camier* acts almost as a parent to *Waiting for Godot*, which, in turn, begets *Endgame*. Bim and Bom (also the names of two Stalinist comedians) are names that appear in the early novel *Murphy* and one of Beckett's last pieces, *What Where*.

Each piece, throughout Beckett's writing career has a familial connection either in theme, appearance or intent. The wild-haired Lucky in *Godot* could be an uncle to the listener in *That Time* whose two brothers appear in *Ohio Impromptu*. Beckett's work forms a huge family tree with each branch informing the others. May in *Footfalls* could be the sister of W in *Rockaby* and so on.

Although made famous by only a handful of pieces, all his work could easily be fused together to make one, huge exploration of humanity. Looking at pieces in an individual way may give a glimpse of what Beckett was about, but the full impact can only really be appreciated when seen as a whole. It is like saying if we look at a single square inch of a Rembrandt portrait we may appreciate the technique, but only by looking at the complete canvas can the full effect be gained.

Waiting for Godot was regarded as only just long enough for a full evening of theatre. Beckett's latter work was even slighter in terms of stage or reading time. Although conceived as individual pieces, they would often be performed in a programme of four or five collected together to make a full theatrical event. The cumulative effect of doing this added further dimensions to what was being presented to the audience.

It could be said that Beckett, like many other artists, hammered mercilessly away on a narrow range of obsessions where other writers would be more expansive, each piece being an entity in its own right. But with Beckett's work there is that cumulative effect in action. His complete work is a 'life' in all its facets. Perhaps it is this that holds him apart from the huge world of literature and dramatic art. He is an artistic peninsular but, boy, what a view there is.

✷ ✷ ✷ ✷ SUMMARY ✷ ✷ ✷ ✷

- Beckett experimented with traditional narrative forms.

- He used the physicality of theatre as well as the text to explore ideas.

- The audience was as much a part of the work as the work itself.

- Every aspect of theatre (stage sets, lighting, action, sound etc.) was used to convey what Beckett wanted to say.

- Beckett was intent on conveying the inner workings of his characters rather than portraying the external action as found in conventional theatre or literature.

- Beckett used the bare minimum in his work – there was no decoration for its own sake.

6 Major themes and techniqes

After meeting Beckett, the composer Morton Feldman, in an interview for *Music and Musicians* (May 1977, p. 5), reported that Beckett said he had only one theme in his life:

> To and fro in shadow, from outer shadow to inner shadow. To and fro, between unattainable self to unattainable non-self.

So how do these themes unravel themselves?

FUTILITY

Pointless communication

As we have seen, very little actually goes on with Beckett's characters. They bicker, argue, fight and generally occupy time with irrelevance. Didi and Gogo in *Godot* come across as a belligerent Tweedledum and Tweedledee, Hamm and Clov are a bleak version of Steptoe and Son and May in *Footfalls* just paces the stage until she finally evaporates.

Beckett had a fascination with the apparent pointlessness of actions. His characters become obsessive over small details (Gogo and his boots, Molloy and his sucking stones etc.). He ponders over the inconsequential details in the lives of his characters rather than taking on grand themes. Yet, those grand themes of life, relationships and existence are addressed in a very human fashion. Beckett's work explores the universe in a grain of sand.

His characters relate to each other in these small ways. The relationship between Reader and Listener in *Ohio Impromptu* is very tangible even though the reader just reads and the listener just listens – the only communication between them being the punctuating wraps on the table from Listener. This is an absurd situation yet how many of us do communicate in ways that would be alien to an onlooker?

Beckett's characters have very definite inner worlds and relationships that the audience is not privy to. The audiences are voyeurs to this world and the characters' dilemmas. It is almost too painful to engage in *Footfalls* or *Rockaby*, yet the situation is compelling. A little like over-hearing an argument or disagreement in a pub or café.

Obsessions

Beckett utilizes the way people each have their own obsessions and idiosyncratic means of communicating. The nakedness that is Beckett's theatre exposes and amplifies the absurdity he sees in the world about him. In a perverse way his work is probably more naturalistic and realistic, in terms of realizing emotions, than the mainstream theatre being produced in his time. Mainstream theatre contrived scenarios to fit the conventions of the stage, thus the productions could only be an impression of reality. Beckett contrived the stage to fit his 'real' portrayal of character. He made the theatre fit reality. In that way, his work was only 'absurd' in terms of theatrical conventions and not in terms of the work itself (unlike Jarry's *Ubu Roi* for instance).

Exhaustion

Together with this there is an underlying weariness with Beckett's characters. Certainly in pieces like *Endgame*, *Krapp's Last Tape* and *Footfalls* there is a pervading sense of running out of energy at the end of a long journey. At this point the vulnerability of the situation and of the characters becomes exposed. Even with the vehement denials and panic with Mouth in *Not I* the fragility of the emotions gives the piece its potency.

The idiocy of being

Why are we here and what is our purpose? This question has been plaguing man for centuries. Beckett explores this and adds a variation by having his characters ask the additional question, since we're here, what shall we do? Thus his characters engage in small, seemingly insignificant activities.

With any form of writing, art or music anything that is placed in front of the audience has a significance. The artist has selected the actions or images in a considered way. A lot of drama has grand, sweeping actions where the audience can concentrate on the big incidents. In Osbourne's *Look Back In Anger*, the angst is big, loud and very physical. It is emotionally charged with a nuclear force. In comparison, Beckett has boots removed or spools changed or chairs being rocked. Yet, the emotional power is just as potent.

LIFE/DEATH

Vladimir: Astride of a grave and a difficult birth. Down in the hole, linger-
            ingly, the gravedigger puts on the forceps.

Waiting For Godot, Faber and Faber (1986), Act 2

Beckett set his work in the hinterland between life and death, although he probably saw his work lying between birth and death. He lit the stage in dramatic fashion and utilized darkness in an almost physical way.

The point between two worlds

John Fletcher looks at how this use of light is explored in *Krapp's Last Tape*:

> The contrast between the fully lit area and the part left in deep shadow is most striking, pinpointing the use of only a very small part of the stage for most of the action, and it is also of dramatic importance. It justifies Krapp's turning round anxiously once or twice as if, Beckett told Martin Held, 'Old Nick' were there: 'Death is standing behind him...'
>
> J. Fletcher, *Faber Critical Guides: Samuel Beckett*,
> Faber and Faber (2000), p. 359

Beckett's work occupies that moment before death; death in the sense of absolute nothingness. The trilogy takes us up to that point, *Endgame* occupies it and *Play* repeats it infinitely.

Beckett enjoyed exploring this narrow band of existence. It gave freedom to his expression. Gone are the fripperies of life. All the characters have left is their essence of their being.

The survivalist nature of character

Despite this dark, almost terminal outlook, Beckett's people were survivors. Either through fear, cowardice or inertia they persevered. In his work there is the spectre of death or approaching death, but overall Beckett leaves the audience with a feel of eternity. *Play* actually repeats, *Not I* fades away without ending, *Endgame* ends with a **tableau**.

KEY TERM

Tableau: A point of frozen time during or at the end of a drama. A static moment presented on stage.

Many of Beckett's final lines tell of an ongoing process. *The Unnamable* ends with:

> I can't go on, I'll go on.

Waiting for Godot ends with:

Vladimir: Well? Shall we go?
Estragon: Yes, let's go.
[*They do not move*]

Rough for Radio II ends:

A: Tomorrow, who knows, we may be free.

Despite the situations that Beckett places his characters, they persist with their predicaments. Suicide or a premature termination of the situation is never an option. Even in *Godot*, Act 1, where Gogo and Didi discuss hanging themselves from the tree, they talk themselves out of it. The sequence ends with:

Vladimir: Well, what do we do?
Estragon: Don't let's do anything. It's safer.

WAITING/TIME

For Beckett, time was an important part of his palette. *Godot* uses time, and the effect of time, to make the process of waiting tangible. He fills time with seeming trivia as in *The Unnamable* that gives the reader the feeling of the weight of time. Beckett turns time into a means of punishment in *Play* with the repeats.

Beckett never fixed time. With his work there is no definite beginning or end, as there is none for us, except birth and death (even then, the finality of this may be disputed by many religious beliefs).

Theodor Adorno comments on Beckett's use of time

> Dostoevski's messianic Prince Mishkin once forgot his watch because no earthly time was valid for him; for Beckett's characters, Mishkin's antithesis, time can be lost because time would contain hope.
>
> T. Adorno, *Trying to Understand Endgame*, Columbia
> University Press (1991), p. 241

ALIENATION

Because of the way Beckett uses the dark and bleak atmosphere of his theatre, the characters appear isolated and alien. They expose their fears in an intimate way to the audience as if calling from the wilderness, backed by settings adrift from reality, almost in a dream state.

This unsettling quality reinforces the overall effects of the text. Beckett reflects his own feelings about alienation – he avoided crowded places and stayed shy of the media – in his texts. He never wrote crowd scenes and used only the bare minimum of actors needed. This left the stage open, making the characters appear more vulnerable.

THE SELF AND MEMORY

Seeing the self

What we are presented with in Beckett's work is humanity with all the trappings pared back to the bare minimum. By doing this he was able to explore what it was to be truly human and to get a glimpse of the 'self'. Since his experience of psychotherapy in London he was fascinated by the roots of personality. This can be seen in the novel trilogy where the personality of the protagonists (or the personalities of the protagonist) is progressively honed into invisibility.

With his later work Beckett's characters are almost ethereal, the self being almost the only thing to be present. He uses only the slightest of signifiers to present to the audience a comprehensible whole. In this way Beckett focuses on his themes with the least distractions.

Remembering and identity

Beckett was fascinated by the essence of humanity and memories. His work has a melancholy air of remembering and nostalgia. Because his characters seem to be looking back at what has happened and the path that has led them to their present condition, the air is imbued with gentle regret. Beckett made the heavy-hearted sigh physically tangible.

With *Godot*, the protagonists use memory to give a perspective to their present condition. The same happens in *Endgame* but it has a more global feel than the personalized memories of Gogo and Didi.

In *Not I* the memories are used as a means of punishment and regret. In a similar, and more affectionate way, Krapp does the same. With *Krapp's Last Tape* the memories are turned into physical entities by being recorded onto tape.

In the trilogy memory is the only means of presenting any form of existence. Throughout Beckett's work, memory is used as a structure to base the present on. The future is never touched on directly, only hinted at in terms of release:

> ... then I could stop, I'd be he, I'd be the silence, I'd be back in the silence, we'd be reunited, his story the story to be told, but he has no story, it's not certain, he's in his own story, unimaginable, unspeakable, that doesn't matter, the attempt must be made, in the old stories incomprehensibly mine, to find this it must be somewhere, it must have been mine, before being this, I'll recognise it, in the end I'll recognise it, the story of the silence that he never left, that I may never find again, that I may find again, then it will be he, it will be I, it will be the place, the silence, the end, the beginning, the beginning again ...

> *The Unnamable*, Picador (1980), p. 380

There is a Native-American saying that states that we travel through life backwards. We can see the past clearly as it goes into the distance. The present can be viewed by looking left and right but the future cannot be seen. This notion helps to give shape to Beckett's drama .

TECHNIQUE

The world stripped bare and the anonymity of setting

Beckett treats his settings in the same way as the characters. He pares back the layers of unnecessary distractions so they are imbued with only the most essential traits. In the trilogy he systematically darkens down the setting from an open landscape through a claustrophobic room to a final oblivion. We can see the same progression from *Godot* through *Endgame* to his later pieces like *Footfalls* where the play is suspended in near total darkness.

The progression of the work of Beckett in this way is similar to the Cheshire cat in Lewis Carroll's *Alice's Adventures Underground*. The most distinctive essence of the cat is its wide, enigmatic smile. Before total invisibility the cat sheds everything until only that broad grin is left. *Not I* parallels this.

By doing this, not only does Beckett turn the spotlight on exactly what he is searching for but he also makes his work universal. There is nothing to place his work in a specific place or time. There are pointers in *Godot* that give some clues to a specific location, as with his early novel, *Murphy*, which is set in London, but these were dispensed with as his work matured.

No past

In Beckett's latter work, all signs of life outside of the play itself were eliminated. The settings are anonymous and free from any symbolic influence outside of the stage and the duration of performance. The characters do not have recognizable names and their dress is devoid of cultural reference. The plays are completely self-contained, the life of the drama can only exist during its time on stage.

By doing this Beckett's work has a timeless quality. With this freedom, the work becomes relevant to the human only and not to culture, history or specific society. As mime can cross boundaries because of the removal of language, so Beckett achieves the same effect with the removal of the trappings of culture and society.

'No matter' – the dismissive element in search of the essence

A little phrase that follows Beckett through his whole canon is 'no matter'. This phrase is uttered almost as punctuation. As Beckett's characters sift through their memories and experience, the phrase takes on a significance beyond its meaning. It can be seen as a change of gear. As his characters decide what is not worthy in their search for a truth in their situation, so 'no matter' acts as a point of waste disposal or reappraisal. Brian Finch comments on this when he says:

> ... each turn of phrase could annul all the sentences that preceded it ... immediately contradicting and then repeated again, and so on.

> B. Finch, *Dimensions, Structures, Textualité dans la Trilogie de Beckett*, Lettres Modernes – Minard (1997), p. 92

By a process of thesis and antithesis, statement and contradiction Beckett both affirms and denies any search for meaning both within his work and within the world beyond.

Precise direction and freedom of interpretation

Because his work uses language in dominance over action, and the actions and movement he uses are precisely documented, his plays work as a text as well as seen in performance. Even the actions, minimal and clearly choreographed and explained, become an element of the text rather than acting as mere instructions. The structure becomes as much a character within the work as the protagonists. A production of *Waiting for Godot* for BBC radio included the stage directions, read by a narrator, as an integral part of the broadcast.

Yet there are huge variations on this. If we take *Not I* as an example, the definitive performance is regarded to be by the actor Billie Whitelaw. It is given at breakneck speed and delivered with the gentlest hint of an Irish accent. But if it is performed at a slower rate, the nature of the

Beckett occupied the crossroads

piece changes. If the accent is changed, the tone of the piece changes. With *Footfalls* the play is performed at a slow and interminable rate. The feeling is overwhelming. Speeded up, it becomes impatient and aggressive allowing a completely different interpretation. Although Beckett was specific over his directions and instructions of his plays, certain details are left open to interpretation. When Beckett states the voices are 'low and slow', how low is low and how slow is slow?

His humour still again shone through with his stage directions. In *Rough for Radio II* he specifies the 'swish of a Bull's Pizzle'. How will we know this, being on radio? Why was he so specific? In *Not I* what exactly is a 'djellaba'? In *Krapp's Last Tape* what is a 'wearish old man'? There are many examples of this throughout his work.

The structure in terms of the medium

Beckett was never content with writing alone. That is, he never wrote for a particular medium using it merely as a platform for his words alone. With *Eh Joe*, a piece written for television, he used the intimacy of the camera to convey the claustrophobia (mental and physical) surrounding the central character. The voiceover, reading the text of the piece, presents itself as the antagonist. This combined effect could only be produced on this small, intimate medium.

With *Film*, Beckett employed the narrative techniques of the cinema to produce the tension between the pursued and the pursuer. *Embers*, written for the radio, employs sound effects to enhance the narrative. *Words and Music*, another piece for the radio, uses music as a defined character within the action. The music interacts with the text in an emotional way.

For his theatre work, Beckett used the space and dynamics of the performance area to add dimensions to his work. In *Not I* the speaking actor is suspended in the space, *Footfalls* uses the tension of the stage edge and the movement to and fro at the division between audience and action, and in *Happy Days* the tableau quality of the stage is exploited.

Beckett plumbed the subconscious

✳ ✳ ✳ ✳ SUMMARY ✳ ✳ ✳ ✳

- Beckett explored the uncomfortable areas of existence.

- Beckett's work inhabits the never-never land between life and death.

- The structure of Beckett's work was as important as the text.

- Beckett rarely had an exact ending to his work. He conveyed the experience of continued presence beyond the fall of the curtain.

- Beckett personified the subconscious

7 Contemporary views of Beckett

A GLOBAL SETTING

In the 1940s, 1950s and 1960s the world was being changed by a cauldron of artistic experimentation and breakthrough, shifting political scenarios and a greater political awareness. Although the technological age had slowed in its dramatic mechanical development, the world was still shifting and evolving in terms of thought, ideas and society.

Beckett's work proved enigmatic

MUSIC

Music, both 'classical' and 'popular' was going through a change. The American **experimental musicians** such as John Cage, Steve Reich, La Monte Young were pushing the boundaries of sound exploration in terms of 'classical music'. John Cage had written extensively for his prepared piano (a piano with objects wedged strategically between the strings turning the instrument into a truly percussive instrument). Terry Riley was experimenting with looped instrumentation and collages of sound. Philip Glass was setting out on his minimal journey of musical textures. Popular music had just turned into rock and roll. Over the following couple of decades this fledgling youth culture of music would go through quantum leaps of change.

VISUAL ART

The **Surrealists** in art were still raising eyebrows with their visual work after taking over the mantel from **Dadaism**. **American abstraction** and **pop art** were not too far away. Experimentation in film was starting to make its presence felt, again, mainly in America and Canada. The new medium of video was becoming available to a wider public.

In the 1960s, an explosion of performance pieces colloquially known as **happenings** amused the gallery goers. The artist Jean Tinguely was constructing huge, pointless machines. Andy Warhol and his Factory employed a multimedia approach – painting,

KEY TERMS

Experimental musicians: A development of music gaining prominence in the 1940s onwards. The conventional forms of music-making, musical notation and musical performance were challenged and experimented with. The major exponents being John Cage, La Monte Young, Terry Riley and Philip Glass.

The Surrealists: A group of artists that moved away from Dada. They used notions of the subconscious to create their images. The major exponents include Salvador Dali, Rene Magritte and Yves Tanguy.

Dadaism: An art group started in Germany at the end of the First World War. It reacted to the carnage of the war and the political landscape. It took an anarchistic approach which caused outrage. The major exponents include Tristan Tzara, Andre Breton and Max Ernst.

American abstraction: Art movement from America that explored the abstracted form of painting rather than a representation of image. Major exponents include Jackson Pollock and Mark Rothko.

film, sex, drugs and rock 'n' roll. The international group **Fluxus** was breaking the rules of artistic convention with great aplomb.

The boundaries of art were being eaten away and one discipline started to merge into another. Music was becoming performance, performance was becoming theatre and theatre was becoming art. All very confusing and very exhilarating. Art was now a huge category. It was becoming harder to define artists by simple categories.

AN UNSETTLED WORLD

The post-war period was an unsettled time. The Korean War gave way to the Vietnam War which left the way for the Cambodian War. The Middle East was an unsettled area. There was the Cold War between America and Russia. Public protestation was a common sight (the Hungarian uprising, the Campaign for Nuclear Disarmament, student riots in Paris in 1968 etc.).

The global picture from the Second World War onwards was one of huge change and uncertainty. The world was a troubled and fearful place. Even the hippie movement in the late 1960s killed itself off in protest against the media narcissism surrounding it. Although Beckett never troubled himself too much with the outside world, he was still aware of the **paradigm shift** that the planet was in. This awareness added tone to his work. It also meant that his work would have a platform and a background to start to reach out to his audience.

KEY TERMS

Pop Art: Art movement started in America where the artist uses icons from popular culture to make their work. The major exponents include Andy Warhol and Roy Lichtenstein.

Happenings: Slang term for spontaneous artistic events, dating from the 1960s. The happening could be a performance of poetry or dance, protest, music, body painting etc. Anything that just happened.

Fluxus: Literally meaning change. An international collective of artists, musicians, writers and filmmakers that explored experimental art and the cross-fertilisation between genres. The major exponents include John Cage, Yoko Ono and George Maciunas.

Paradigm shift: A movement away from the traditional or established rules. Relates to major, global change in thought or action.

REACTION TO BECKETT'S PRE-*GODOT* WORK

As with any fledgling writer, the first footings into the world are lined with disappointments. Apart from his essay on Proust and a few poems published in literary magazines Beckett did not gain much recognition from his early work.

It was only with the publication of the first part of his trilogy, *Molloy*, in 1951 that the wider circles started to take notice. Then, in 1953, after the effort of his wife and the actor/director Roger Blin, *Waiting for Godot* exploded into the world. After that, Beckett's reputation was secured and 20 years of sticking to his guns against all odds had paid off. *Godot* was first performed on 5 January 1953. Beckett was 46 years old.

THEATRE OF THE ABSURD

Parisian theatre

In the twentieth century, Parisian theatre fitted into three groups. First, there were the subsidised houses for 'classic' theatre. Second there were the theatres on the boulevards that were commercial concerns handling adult comedies and 'problem' plays. Third there were the small, independent 'pocket theatres' that handled the more adventurous and experimental theatre.

Changes

The theatre of Paris in the 1920s was already being shaken from a naturalistic complacency by the **Futurists** who broke all the theatrical rules with their short plays about the machine age. The Dada group was being outrageous in Germany and France with their cabarets and performance events. The style of theatre was changing and this helped inform the way Beckett worked. What Beckett was doing with his writing was not radically new, but it did cross boundaries and offer the mainstream theatre a more palatable snippet of the **avant-garde**.

KEY TERMS

Futurists: An art movement started in Italy in 1906 to celebrate the machine age and replacing traditional aesthetics.

Avant-garde: Any artist, writer or musician etc. whose techniques or ideas are experimental and ahead of their time. Artists whose work is radical or daring.

It was in the small theatres that the Absurdists found a home and in which *Godot* first saw the light of day. The playwright Eugéne Ionesco, in an essay on Franz Kafka first published in 1957, defined the Absurd as:

> ... that which is devoid of purpose ... cut off from his religious, meta-physical, and transcendental roots, man is lost; all of his actions become senseless, absurd, useless.

> M. Esslin, *The Theatre of the Absurd*, Penguin (1991), p. 23

This, broadly speaking, is the concern of Beckett.

An accidental dramatist

Although Beckett is connected with the Theatre of the Absurd, this tag never really existed beyond a loose pigeon-hole. The exponents of the absurd never collected together in a cohesive group outside of passing friendships.

Beckett had fallen into theatre almost by accident. His first foray into playwriting began with an abandoned play about Samuel Johnson, followed by *Elutheria*, written in 1947 which was a reasonably conventional affair compared to *Godot*. *Eluthenia* was never performed and Beckett insisted that it was scratched from his canon of work. It is only recently that it has been available in printed form.

The absurd writers

The main exponents of this class of theatre never knew each other outside of acquaintances, and were not the coherent group that, say, the Surrealists were. The title, applied by Martin Esslin in 1961, covered quite a wide range. Some of the main exponents included the Italian Luigi Pirandello (1867–1936. *Six Characters in Search of an Author*); Franco-Romanian leading light of the Absurd, Eugène Ionesco (1912–1994, *The Bald Soprano, The Chairs*); Spanish painter and giant of the arts Pablo Picasso – yes, *that* Picasso – (1881–1973, *Desire Caught by the Tail*) and the American Edward Albee (1928–, *The American Dream, Who's Afraid of Virginia Woolf*). Others associated with this strand of theatre include Jean Genet and Harold Pinter. The notion of Absurdity spread far throughout Europe embracing writers such as Günter Grass and Vaclav Havel.

All of these writers explored similar themes that fit the definition from Ionesco above. They also had a similar presentation – stark stage, few characters, minimal props. This is possibly explained (somewhat cynically but ultimately practically) by Ionesco again:

> The reason why Absurdist plays take place in No Man's Land with only two characters is primarily financial.
>
> J. Law *et al.* (eds), *The Companion to Theatre*, Cassell (1997), p. 46

Like all experimental or avant-garde art, finances were limited and everybody had to muck in. With the first run of *Godot* both director Roger Blin and Beckett went without pay.

The small theatres that housed the plays were very basic only holding 200 people at the most. Many were running on the breadline. They were mainly clustered around the Montparnasse region of Paris snuggled close to the cafés. It was to this environment that Beckett first came into the public's attention beyond the literary clique he was used to thus far.

MINIMALIST WRITING

Beckett's style and his mix of the avant-garde and music-hall themes caused confusion and perplexed audiences when *Waiting for Godot* was premiered. With a bare stage (apart from a bleak tree, a mound and a road), two 'tramps' (who do very little but wait) and three other passing characters, his play was difficult to digest for the contemporary, mainstream theatre goer. The comment from the critic Vivian Mercier that this is a play where 'nothing happens, twice' was perfectly understandable.

GODOT ARRIVES IN FRANCE, ENGLAND AND SAN QUENTIN PENITENTIARY

Although the public were used to the smaller theatres performing strange theatrical effects they were not quite ready for Beckett who, somehow, slipped into the mainstream.

Paris in the late 1940s was still a hotbed of the arts. Although most of the Surrealists had moved to America after the war, their influence was still strong. Picasso was never far away and Sartre and Camus were philosophizing in the cafés. Jean Cocteau was making his films and the avant-garde dramatists such as Ionesco, Artaud and Adamov were filling the stage.

A SHAKY START

That being said, *Godot* had a fair run of rejections until the actor/director Roger Blin took the work on board. It took three years to beg and borrow the money to perform the play. It finally hit the stage of the Théâtre de Babylone on 4 January 1953. In this first performance Pierre Latour played Estragon, the cabaret star Lucien Raimbourg played Vladimir, Jean Martin played Lucky and Blin, himself, played Pozzo.

The French critics could see the worth of his work but remained a bit perplexed as to what it was exactly *about*. In *L'Aurore* (6 January 1953), G. Joly, inaccurately, wrote:

> This unusual work by the American novelist seems to be inspired by the miserable condition of famished tramps hunted down by farmers, who abound in the South of the United States.

Luc Estang wrote in *La Croix* (9 January 1953) of the general themes in the play as:

> ... the absurdity of the human condition, useless freedom, human resignation, and on top of it the delusion of hope.

Robert Kemp of *La Monde* (14 January 1953) offered lukewarm praise when he wrote:

if the play shows no genius, however, it is nevertheless full of good will.

Overall, the reception by the French press ranged from tepid to enthusiastic, no one was overtly hostile. Jacques Lemarchand in Figaro Littéraire (17 January 1953) went as far as to say that Godot:

> indicates the true direction of a whole dramatic movement that is still in a period of research.

In its first run, directed by Blin, the play achieved 400 performances and captured the imagination of the audience. The American director Alan Schneider summed it up as; 'Godot had me in the beginnings of a grip from which I have never escaped' ('Waiting for Beckett', *The Chelsea Review*, September 1958.)

According to Martin Esslin, over a million people had seen it in its first five years and it was being performed all over Europe. Because of this popularity the play slipped into the conventional theatre almost by the back door.

Godot had an immediate effect on other writers such as Jean Anouilh and Allain Robbe-Grillet. Bertold Brecht even wanted to write a counter play to Godot with Estragon as a proletarian, Vladimir as an intellectual, Pozzo as a landowner and Lucky as a fool or policeman(!). In 1966 the playwright, Miodrag Bulatovic, wrote *Godot Arrived*. Here, Godot not only turned up but was a baker.

PERPLEXITY

If anything it was the humanity of his pieces that stopped them being merely experimental and off the wall. He made a connection to the audience with the flashes of tenderness that seemed to spring from nowhere.

Estragon: Don't touch me!
[*Vladimir holds back, pained.*]
Vladimir: Do you want me to go away? [*Pause.*] Gogo! [*Pause. Vladimir observes him attentively.*] Did they beat you? [*Pause.*] Gogo! [*Estragon remains silent, head bowed.*] Where did you spend the night?

Estragon:	Don't touch me! Don't question me! Don't speak to me! Stay with me!
Vladimir:	Did I ever leave you?
Estragon:	You let me go.
Vladimir:	Look at me! [*Estragon does not raise his head. Violently.*] Will you look at me!

[*Estragon raises his head. They look long at each other, then suddenly embrace, clapping each other on the back. End of the embrace. Estragon, no longer supported, almost falls.*]

Waiting for Godot, Faber and Faber (1986), Act 2, p. 54

It was probably these flashes of tenderness, interspersed between the slapstick, cruelty and nonsense that unsettled and intrigued the first audiences.

ENGLAND'S RESERVE

If the French critics were mildly perplexed, then the conservative English theatre was bamboozled. At that time English theatre tradition was set in the naturalistic tradition and the new theatre emerging in the 1950s was the one of the angry young man at his angry kitchen sink.

Into this world came Beckett. His work was neither naturalistic nor realistic in a traditional, theatrical sense and he was never willing to compromize for the English audience. His work was truly shocking. Not because of the language (John Osbourne used stronger, more confrontational words) or because it was anti-establishment (Joe Orton grabbed that pigeon-hole) but because it broke the mould of convention. *Endgame* caused even more problems for the English censor who did not like the idea of God being referred to as a bastard (Beckett did make a compromise here and changed the offending word to 'swine'). The opening night of *Endgame* was described in the *Times* newspaper in 1967 as, 'a rather horrible evening'.

The critics, in general, were initially hostile. The national papers intoned to the effect 'The Left Bank can keep it!' (J. Knowlson, *Damned to Fame*, Bloomsbury (1997), p. 415). Cecil Wilson commented that: 'this [Godot] is tedious' and Milton Shulman said that *Godot* was:

'another of those plays that tries to lift superficiality to significance through obscurity' (Ibid.).

It was not until the heavyweight critics Kenneth Tynan and Harold Hobson waded in that fortunes for *Godot* changed. Where as before people were walking out by the end of Act 1, now this curiosity from the exiled Irishman caught the theatre going public's imagination. Hobson wrote of Godot that, '...at the best something...will securely lodge in a corner of your mind for as long as you live.' (Ibid, p. 415).

Beckett soon found himself in a curious position. He was thought to be too off the wall for conventional theatre goers. They tended to blanche at his offerings. But equally he was regarded as too mainstream by the avant-garde. Neither house was willing to embrace Beckett with open arms. Even today, Beckett sits under this artistic road sign, neither in one place or the other. One suspects that this state of affairs would have amused Beckett greatly.

AN IDEAL AUDIENCE

Yet despite this hostility something obviously struck a chord. In a noted performance of *Godot* in San Quentin Penitentiary in 1957 the prisoners immediately recognized what Beckett was saying. The inmates were world authorities on waiting. Where the critics had puzzled and cogitated themselves into knots, the prisoners immediately made satisfying connections.

As Martin Esslin postulates in *The Theatre of the Absurd*:

> Or perhaps because they [the prisoners] were unsophisticated enough to come to the theatre without any preconceived notions and ready-made expectations, so that they avoided the mistake that trapped so many established critics who condemned the play for its lack of plot, development, characterisation, suspence, or plain common sense.

> M. Esslin, *The Theatre of the Absurd*, Penguin (1991), p. 21

The reaction of the prisoners to Beckett's work gives a clear signpost that his work calls for an emotional reaction rather than an academic one, although there are many tantalizing allusions in his text to keep the academic happy.

ATTRACTING AND ALARMING ACTORS

Despite the unconventionality of the play it was appreciated in its time and attracted many well-known actors to perform his work such as the famous French actress Madelene Renaud, who played Winnie in *Happy Days*.

But, unlike in France, the cream of English actors tended to steer clear of Beckett. Whether they thought it was a bad career move or not, they tended to give him a wide berth. Sir John Gielgud turned down *Endgame* stating in the *Sunday Times* (24 September 1961) that he, 'couldn't stand it or understand it'. Sir Ralph Richardson turned down the role of Estragon after Beckett refused to explain what the character of Pozzo represented. Richardson later expressed his regret at this decision, recognizing that he was taking the work of Beckett too literally.

This, though, was not the whole story. Because of delays in the production and the interference of the Lord Chamberlain's censorship, both Richardson and Alec Guinness (who was to star in the production as well) had other arrangements. This had a knock-on effect for the opening in America where Buster Keaton had been lined up to play Vladimir and Marlon Brando had been ear marked to play Estragon. None of these actors could appear in the productions.

When the comedian, Max Wall, agreed to perform *Godot* in the 1970s his agent was allegedly appalled and tried to convince him not to do it. As it turned out, Wall's Vladimir was a huge success and, if anything, enhanced his career.

Bert Lahr, who played the cowardly lion in *The Wizard of Oz*, received a letter from Tennessee Williams after a production of *Godot* in 1956. It raged:

> … how can the man, who has charmed the youth of America as the lion

in the Wizard of Oz, appear in a play which is communistic, atheistic, and existential?

A. Cronin, *The Last Modernist*, Flamingo (1997), p. 445

Dame Peggy Ashcroft played Winnie in *Happy Days* in 1976 when the play opened at the National Theatre in London's South Bank complex, although she nearly did not when Beckett's meticulous directions in rehearsal tried the patience of the great actress to the limit.

HOME OF THE NOT SO FAMOUS

It was only relatively unknown actors who performed in English productions. Both Patrick Magee and Billie Whitelaw made their careers by performing, under Beckett's guidance, definitive performances of the work. It is only in recent years that better known actors such as Ben Kingsley and John Hurt embraced Beckett's text.

Although his work has proved popular, no piece has sustained a major run on Broadway or in the major London theatres. Although lauded as a literary giant and great innovator, the majority of the population has probably never seen any of Beckett's work. The title of *Godot* is part of our language, yet it holds a place just outside our consciousness. Beckett perplexes the world and the world acts in a perplexing way in return. Once again Beckett sits at a crossroads.

✳ ✳ ✳ *SUMMARY* ✳ ✳ ✳

- Beckett made a bridge between the avant-garde and the mainstream theatre.

- Beckett fell foul of the censor and poor reviews.

- Actors were either intrigued or repelled by Beckett's dramas.

- The artistic world was going through rapid change.

- Beckett refused, or at least resented, compromize in his work or productions.

- Initial hostility changed to muted respect as the critics were slowly won over.

- Well-known comics were willing to 'risk' their reputations for Beckett.

- Beckett brought the Theatre of the Absurd to a wide audience.

Modern critical approaches to Beckett

8

BECKETT TODAY

As we gain some distance from Beckett since his death in 1989 and we become more familiar with his work it *should* become easier to get a clearer perspective of the man and his writing and its place in modern literary theory.

Although still shocking, intriguing and challenging, Beckett's work is not so alien to us now. Beckett's experimentation is comprehensible in terms of contemporary art and theatre, and his explorations of the subconscious and behaviour are now a well-travelled path. What is happening today is a re-evaluation of his work in terms of academic study, and there is much for the academics to get their teeth into.

THE REACTION OF ACADEMIA

There are millions of words conjecturing the meaning of Beckett's work; as there are many academics so there are as many interpretations. Commentators such as James Knowlson, Beckett's biographer, react strongly against the whole process of academic interpretation

> Some critics have over-intellectualised Beckett, ignoring his own protestations that he was not a philosopher, for instance, and a view that treats the plays as if they were philosophical tracts given a top-dressing of theatrical fertilizer is doomed to failure.

> Interview in *Independent*, December 26 1989

This would certainly have been Beckett's view. His reaction to early reviews of *Godot* was that he, 'was tired of the whole thing and the endless misunderstandings. Why people have to complicate a thing so simple I can't make out' (J. Knowlson, 1997, *Damned to Fame*, Bloomsbury, p. 416).

Whether such efforts are doomed to failure or not, the interest of academics in Beckett's work shows no sign of abating.

POLITICAL READINGS

Beckett was not a political animal in the way that his contemporary Bertholt Brecht was. Beckett made no overtures in his writing to any one political idiom, yet his work, by its very nature, was one of struggle. It is possible to interpret his characters in such a way as to make them correspond to a particular line of political thought; look, for example, at Brecht's reworking of *Godot* or the attempts to equate the play with Christian notions of redemption.

Given the sense of oppression that is so often current in Beckett's work it is not surprising that it has attracted considerable comment from Marxist theorists. The relationships in many of Beckett's dramatic works can be seen in terms of both power and class. This can be seen in the relationships between Pozzo and Lucky in *Godot* and Hamm and Clov in *Endgame*. Peter Boxall comments:

> The mutual exclusivity between an East European commitment to Socialist realism, and a Western emphasis on artistic autonomy and apoliticism, keeps Ivan [referring to Solzhenitzyn's character Ivan Denisovich in the eponymous *A Day in the Life of* ...] and Clov locked up in their respective 'shelters' as effectively as do Stalin and Hamm.

> P. Boxall, *Waiting for Godot/Endgame: A Reader's Guide to Essential Criticism*, Icon Books (2000), p. 140

NO SOLUTIONS

Commentators do recognize the dilemma of finding labels for Beckett. Rosemary Pountney expresses it thus:

> Unlike Brecht, who believed that to present a problem on the stage presented also an implied solution, in the desirability of social change, Beckett has no solution to offer. Nor does he believe that it is the task of the artist to provide any.

> R. Pountney, *Theatre of Shadows: Samuel Beckett's Drama 1956–76*, Colin Smythe (1988), p. 194

This is part of the problem: that what Beckett seems to do is provide considerable insight into the problem of the human condition but equally he fails to offer a solution, particularly one that commends a particular political standpoint. Beckett's skill was to paint in very visual terms a particular scene; he seemed less interested in offering any analysis of his creation.

Beckett is difficult to pigeon hole

As Catherine Belsey and others have argued, the traditional forms of the realist novel (such as chronological time-schemes, psychologically identifiable characters and intricate plotting) tend to encourage a conventional view of the world, if only because they leave our assumptions about it unchallenged. By the same token those such as Beckett who reject such convention can be seen as producing, as Peter Barry puts it, 'a response to the contradictions and diversions inherent in late capitalist society.' (P. Barry, 1995, *Beginning Theory*, Manchester University Press, p. 159). In this sense Beckett's claims to be apolitical can be seen as disingenuous. The very form that he uses, the disjointed, fragmented style, the lack of definite beginnings, middles and ends, can be seen in itself as a political comment on the society it represents.

FEMINISM

Is Beckett gender neutral? Beckett wrote for women as well as men, specifying gender type in his plays, yet his themes were not particularly gender specific. Someone new to his work might comment on the starkness and bleakness of the work and its apparent lack of the redeeming 'feminine' characteristics of caring and compassion, but in general the overt themes might seem to be gender neutral. However, Beckett's writing does have specific areas of interest for feminist theorists. Some of his plays have central female characters, such as *Happy Days*, *Not I* or *Footfalls* where the emotions explored in the piece relate directly to the concerns of the female – with *Not I*, where rape and illegitimate birth are hinted at and *Footfalls* which explores a mother–daughter relationship.

Lack of female presence

However, overall, it is the very lack of female characters, such as in *Waiting for Godot*, which causes interest. Mary Bryden identifies Beckett's 'erasure of specificity from gender patterning' and goes on to warn that Beckett 'runs the risk of attracting accusations of tolerating that phenomenon of female "invisibility"...' (M. Bryden, 'Gender in Transition', in *Waiting for Godot: Repretition, Theory and Text*, ed. S Connor, Blackwell (1988), p. 62)

Her main argument revolves around this absence of the feminine, and concludes that:

> the slackening hold on gender determinism which these plays [*Waiting for Godot* and *Endgame*] display points forward to a succession of later drama and prose in which gender as a categoriser retreats, along with other organising categories, to cede to the all-encompassing quest of the fragmenting yet persisting self.

Ibid. p. 156

Women and guilt

Certainly we can see that the moment of birth, essentially a female issue, is reduced to mechanics in *Waiting for Godot*.

> **KEY TERM**
>
> Feminism: The study of gender politics from a female perspective.

> Astride of a grave and a difficult birth ... The air is full of our cries.
>
> *Waiting for Godot*, Faber and Faber (1986), Act 2, p. 84

This might seem to be inclusive but the lack of humanity in the bleak image negates any sense of a woman giving birth. Feminists might argue that this image of giving birth astride a grave is also linked directly back to the myth of the Fall.

Sarah Bryant-Bertail comments:

> The topography in *All That Fall* is distinctly hostile to the females – human or animal – who try to walk through it. Maddy's comment 'It is suicide to be a broad' suggests that her death will be her own fault, namely the fault of being a woman.
>
> S. Bryant-Bertail, *The True-Real Woman: Maddy Rooney as Picara in All That Fall*, University of Washington Press (2000), Seattle

The allusion to the Fall in the title of the piece, the fall of grace of Adam and Eve, relates to the once popular notion that the Fall was Eve's fault, and that women have had to carry the burden of that guilt ever since. Beckett can therefore be seen reinforcing that stereotype, by accident if not by intention.

The paradox of genderless writing

Although Beckett was intent on exploring the essence of being human, male/female roles *are* delineated. In *Eh Joe* the figure we see is being talked to by a female voice. In *Happy Days* Winnie is the active figure on stage and her husband Willie is the more passive character. Yet in his later work, Beckett makes gender anonymous, as in *Quad* or *Ohio Impromptu*.

This points to a paradox in Beckett's work. If the work is gender universal, why were men chosen to play all the parts in *Waiting for Godot* in its premieres around the world? And yet if the work is truly genderless in intent and execution, why should we worry?

Certainly there is a need for gender to be specified in relation to the text in some of Beckett's plays – but what, if anything, would be lost or distorted, say, if Krapp were played by a woman or a man played Mouth in *Not I*?

RELIGIOUS READINGS

Beckett frequently used religious concepts in his work, most noticeably with *Godot* and *Endgame*. His technique would seem to be to take religious doctrine and pull it apart with his keen eye and dry wit. The consternation he provoked with his use of the name Godot demonstrates this.

As with his politics, Beckett never acknowledged an allegiance with any particular religious group. What he did with his writing was be the thorn in the side of religious dogma. He raised issues and put the Church (or suggestions of the Church) in conflict with the everyday. A good example of this was the problems that the Lord Chancellor had with God being called a bastard in *Endgame* when the play first came to England.

One man and his dogma

Beckett was not afraid of causing offence. But his wicked sense of humour could not help but shine through. A man of his intelligence could not be blind to the statements he was making in his work. There was no such thing as a happy accident with Beckett. Everything was thought through meticulously. In a way his education was used as a weapon against his educators. Beckett wanted to get to the heart of the matter, wanted to get to the heart of humanity, and religion was just a stile on his journey.

Even so G. S. Fraser, in his review of *Godot* in the *Times Literary Supplement* (10 February 1956), wrote:

> Their lot is increasing misery; but if Didi and Gogo are not obviously better off at the end of the play than they were at the beginning, neither are they any worse off. Their state remains one of expectation. *Waiting for Godot* – one might sum up these remarks – is thus a modern morality play, on permanent Christian themes.

Even more emphatic, but from an opposite position, is an essay that compares Lucky in *Godot* to Christ:

> Samuel Beckett may have denied the use of Christian mythology in *Waiting for Godot*, but the character of Lucky proves otherwise. We can read Lucky as a symbolic figure of Christ, and, as such, his actions in the play carry a criticism of Christianity, suggesting that the merits of Christianity have decreased to the point where they no longer help man at all.
>
> G. Tigani, *Christ's Body of Evidence*, Yale University Thesis (1988), p. 2

Tigani goes on to conclude that:

> Christ was both the beginning and the end of Christianity, just as Lucky began his service with high intentions, but ends as a slave who speaks only gibberish, on his way to the auction block. In the end, they both destroy what they hoped to create.
>
> Ibid

In citing two such diverse viewpoints we can see another problem with the enigmatic nature of Beckett's work is that he can be used to illuminate the faith of the believer and the denial of the atheist with equal success.

Christianity is not the only religion to be applied to Beckett. In his book, *Nothing Left to Tell*, John Kundert-Gibbs comments that:

> Although the aspects of Zen with which Beckett is most commonly connected is its description of the continuous, cyclical suffering of the world's inhabitants, I believe that his implicit rejection of the logical and the narratively cohesive, as well as the value he places on terseness

and brevity and the sense of imminence and immediacy his plays evoke connect both the form and the underlying intent of his work in profound ways with the tenets of Zen.

> J. L. Kundert-Gibbs, *Nothing Left to Tell: Zen/Chaos Theory in the Dramatic Art of Samuel Beckett*, Associated University Presses (1999), p. 30

In this fascinating if highly complex study Kundert-Gibbs provides a reading of the plays which focuses on the 'lessness' of the works, that is, the idea of minimilization, of the 'nothingness' in the works.

PHILOSOPHICAL AND THEORETICAL READINGS

Much has been made of Beckett's philosophical content. He was a reader of philosophical ideas, enjoying writers such as Arthur Schopenhauer and Immanuel Kant. As with politics and religion, this is a potential trap for a misguided interpretation.

Frustratingly, Beckett's work has a shape that can be fitted into many of the philosophies and theories. Jacques Derrida recognized the problem of trying to analyze Beckett when he wrote:

> This [Beckett] is an author to whom I feel very close, or to whom I would like to feel myself close; but also too close. Precisely because of this proximity, it is too hard for me, too easy and too hard.

> J. Derrida, *Acts of Literature*, Routledge (1999), p. 60

Locating Beckett in theoretical study does prove difficult. Anthony Uhlmann comments on this in his book *Beckett and Poststructuralim*:

> When I ask 'what is literary criticism?' or even, 'what is Beckett studies?', I find myself developing a series of apparently heterogeneous generalisations; whereas in this particular case it seems much more useful to ask 'which one? ... ', which aspects of Beckett? Which aspect of Beckett's work? Which, or what kind of literary criticism? Which Beckett critic?

> A. Ullman, *Beckett and Poststructuralism*, Cambridge University Press (1999), p. 2

Uhlmann looks at a broad range of Beckett's work in relation to a number of recent French Poststructuralist philosophers, focusing particularly on the work of Foucault, Deleuze and Derrida. He looks for example on the question of 'Being', trying to show a resonance between this issue as it is presented by Beckett and similar concerns in contemporary poststructuralist philosophy. He sees the similarity arising from a fact of what amounts to historical necessity:

> If the works of Beckett and philosophers such as Deleuze, Foucault, Serres, Derrida and Levinas have numerous and striking points of intersection, then it is partly because they have encountered or existed within the same non-discursive milieu, that time and place which produced the same series of problems, the same problem-field – the France, emerging from World War Two, of *'la guerre franco-francaise'*.

Ibid, p. 18

THE DECENTRED UNIVERSE

Peter Boxall identifies within Beckett's work a resistance to developments in contemporary thought. He comments:

> Whilst critical discourses are mutating and evolving, finding ever new ways to think about the relation between the text and the world, Beckett criticism has sometimes seemed to draw a protective ring around his work.

P. Boxall, *Waiting for Godot/Endgame: A Reader's Guide to Essential Criticism*, Icon Books (2000), p. 94

Whether it was Beckett's own resistance to analyzing his own work or his obvious distaste for those who attempted the task, there is still a sense of unwillingness at times to engage in the process. Yet the theories of Poststructuralism seem to fit Beckett's own concerns. Poststructuralism takes the **Structuralist** proposition that it is language which shapes our world and considers the consequences of

KEY TERM

Structuralism: In linguistics, any approach to the analysis of language that pays explicit attention to the way in which linguistic features can be described in terms of structures and systems.

this radical idea. If our world is constructed by language then perhaps it is not as tangible as we would like to imagine. Where are the certainties, the fixed points, that can help us work out where we are, even who we are? The Poststructuralists refer to a world which is uncertain and unknown as the **decentred universe**.

LANGUAGE AND LINGUISTICS

This is fine, but Beckett was aware that words carry a whole range of meanings to an audience – that is, they constantly relate to things and so are very difficult to isolate from the audiences experience. Brian Finney suggests that:

> As an avant-garde writer Beckett fretted from the start of his career over the inescapable significance that accompanies the words he wants to use abstractly. In a world deprived of meaning how can the linguistic artist express this meaninglessness with words that necessarily convey meaning? How can he produce what he called a 'literature of the unword?'

> B. Finney, Samuel Beckett's Postmodern Fictions, in *The Columbia History of the British Novel*, ed. J. Ricketti, Columbia University Press (1994), p. 50

And so language becomes a point of issue. There is a strain of philosophy that looks purely at the thought of language. The philosopher Ludwig Wittgenstein is a prime example of this kind of practitioner of philosophy as he explores language above content. This is a problematic area because we get involved with the dilemma of language as representational of action as opposed to the action promoting the need for language. But with Beckett there is much more than mere semantics.

Martin Seymour-Smith, points out that the world of Beckett:

> ... is made peculiarly desolate by his concentration on the solipsist isolation of his characters, who mediate ceaselessly upon their coming

extinction, continuing the while to contemplate language, their only weapon – a useless one.

M. Seymour-Smith, *Guide to Modern World Literature*, Papermac (1986), p. 494

PSYCHOLOGICAL THEORY

Beckett was intrigued by Jung's ideas. Although he synthesized them and adapted them into his own, personal reading of the world, he did not seek out defining theories about what it is to be human, he just reported it. In this sense he was a journalist of the mind. He just put down in words what it was to be alive.

Explorations of memory

In his essay *The Subjective Imperative of Voice: Reflections on Samuel Beckett* Robert Lukehart explains:

> The most recent marriage of opposites in the psychological community refer to two distinctive forms of memory: explicit memory and implicit memory. These may be helpful in understanding the actions and motivations of Beckett's characters since they are products of psychological realism.

Here, the importance of memory, either voluntary or involuntary, becomes a focus of Beckett's work, as it was for Marcel Proust. Obviously memory informs his work, as in *Krapp's Last Tape* and *Not I*. Memory proves a crucial point in the drama. But the memory, in terms of personal history, as presented by Beckett is not necessarily far reaching. For him, memory does not stretch beyond the limits of the piece being presented. Beckett contains memory to the perimeters of the play concerned and not beyond.

Finding a meaning, an answer or a truth?

Both Jung and Freud developed ways of trying to understand the workings of the mind and find answers to the mechanics of the subconscious. Their search was essentially an ontological one whereas Beckett's was, if anything, the opposite. As Martin Seymour-Smith puts it:

In the quest of reason, and finding none, he [Beckett] has elevated pur-
poselessness itself into a reason.

M. Seymour-Smith, *Guide to Modern World Literature*, Papermac
(1986), p. 494

If Beckett does provide an answer it is probably a grim one: that pain
will never be eradicated, and that is potentially his greatest truth.

A WIDER PERSPECTIVE

So where does Beckett sit in the artistic movements of the twenty-first
century? It is possibly too soon to see his exact position in the scheme of
things. As we have seen, he is constantly being revisited and re-evaluated.
But what is emerging is his place in the transition between Modernism
and Postmodernism.

Modernism was a movement that grew out of a changing mechanical
world. It encapsulated this change and broke free from the late-
Romantic period that dominated the nineteenth century. Both James
Joyce and T. S. Eliot shattered the rules of literary convention with their
writing, wilfully casting convention aside. The visual arts were to be
changed for ever with the advent of Picasso, Cubism, Dada (in the
1920s) and Surrealism (in the 1930s).

Into all of this Beckett was drawn. Certainly the Modernist movement
laid the path for Beckett, but where the Modernists ground to a halt so
Beckett took off. Where the new establishment took hold, Beckett
broke free and carried the mantle of artistic exploration forward.

Modern or Postmodern?

In her book *The Painted Word: Samuel Beckett's Dialogue with Art*, Lois
Oppenheim identifies Beckett's position as neither Modern nor
Postmodern but rather something which encompasses both. She sees
him as struggling to overcome a number of what she calls 'dualisms',
including among them mind/body, internal/external and ego/world. In
trying to overcome these oppositions she suggests that Beckett's work
became increasingly self-conscious. She argues that:

... It is the self-consciousness that resulted in the minimalist writing, and the collapse of genre, characteristic of all the late work.

L. Oppenheim, *The Painted Word: Samuel Beckett's Dialogue with Art*, Michigan Press (2000), p. 5

By the time Beckett was producing his mature work, and at the same time becoming well known, all the change in the first part of the century was becoming tired and commonplace. Modernism had changed radically from the euphoria at the turn of the century, through two world wars and a liberalism of ideas, to an almost artistic weariness.

No longer was there a marvel in the new and different. Now there was a reaction against the mixed euphoria of the 'modern' world. Art started to become more personal again. The Romanticism of the previous century was merged with a more overtly political stance. After two horrendous wars, new art began to question and re-evaluate society. It started to search below the surface. Modernism got shunted into a more aware rebellion concentrated on survival rather than progress.

Outside to inside

Whereas the previous decades had skimmed the surface and absorbed the outside so Postmodernism scooped inwards. Beckett's work celebrated and questioned this change. Frank Kermode sums it up thus:

If there is a new *avant-garde* – based, say, on [John] Cage, [William] Burroughs, Beckett and [Jorges Luis] Borges, concrete poetry and the *nouveau roman*, but also on the happening, drugs, the counter-culture, and *négritude* – this is no longer simply a style; it is a form of post-cultural *action*, a politics.

F. Kermode, , *Innovations: Essays on Art and Ideas* (1968), p. 62

While being collected with his contemporaries in all fields of the arts when it came to collating the shifting themes of expression under a single title, Beckett always seemed one step ahead of everybody else. He was Postmodern in the time of Modernism, he *is* contemporary when we are still coming to terms with Postmodernism. Even with the new terms of Neurotic Realism, Re-Modernism and whatever terms are in use today, Beckett can often seem one footfall ahead, not necessarily because of his realizations in terms of actual pieces (writing, drama or art) but because of his freeing of ideas from constraint.

* * * *SUMMARY* * * *

- Beckett is prone to many and varied explanations.

- Beckett's work promotes a very personal response.

- Beckett is seen to be a link between Modernism and Postmodernism.

- Beckett himself was wary and bemused by critical analysis of his work that he thought to be very straightforward.

Where next?

9

There is a great deal more to know about Beckett, his work, his life and his approach to theatre. Because he occupied such a no man's land it is difficult to get a complete picture of the actual impact he had not only on theatre but on such a wide range of the arts in general.

He was a very unique artist quietly working away on his vision regardless of conventions. This is why he was so admired and his influence has had such an impact for so many people from musicians to painters.

Ultimately, the best way to know the man is through his work and that is where anyone should start. If you met him in a little café, over coffee and whisky, smoking Gitanes, you would talk about cricket or chess or anything other than his writing. This he considered was outside of himself and autonomous. If you wanted to be in the company of Beckett you just chatted and had a good time, got drunk and put the world to rights. Then he would wander off through the Parisian streets to a bar that stayed open longer.

BOOKS
There are many books about Beckett. He has spawned an industry of analysis about him (not of his conscious making) and millions of words have been written about his life and his work.

Beckett's work
Naturally, the primary source material is the work of Beckett himself. These are readily available in collected forms. Faber and Faber publish his collected plays and his novel trilogy. Penguin publishes his collected short prose. John Calder publishes his other novels, collected poems and shorter prose. The Grove Press publishes his complete shorter prose. Beckett's work is always in print. Just make sure you look under both fiction and drama, as bookshops seem to be as confused as everyone else about where he should go.

Also available are the *Notebooks of Samuel Beckett* published in various volumes by Faber and Faber. These are quite expensive and are really for the most devoted of devotees. They contain his written sketches of his plays in facsimile form (be warned, his handwriting is difficult to read) but they give a close view of the mechanics of the man.

Biography

There are two excellent biographies of Beckett. The first is *Damned to Fame* by James Knowlson (published by Bloomsbury, 1997). This book is an indispensable encyclopaedia of Beckett. It is very thick and very detailed but lovingly put together.

The next is *The Last Modernist* by Anthony Cronin (published by Flamingo, 1997). Although not as detailed as *Damned to Fame*, it makes a very good, very straight forward read about Beckett, his life and his work. Both of these biographies are indispensable for anyone interested in the subject.

Other books that give an insight into the man are *No Author Better Served*, a collection of letters between Beckett and Alan Schneider (published by Harmon, in hardback, 1998) and *Conversations With (and about) Beckett* by Mel Gusson (published by Nick Herne Books, 2000). Both of these books give an insight into Beckett through reported conversations.

Essays and analysis

Next are the books that give a wider picture. Both Martin Esslin's *The Theatre of the Absurd* (published by Penguin, 1976) and Ruby Cohn's *From Desire to Godot* (published by John Calder, 1999) give a comprehensive insight into the Theatre of the Absurd and the environment that Beckett emerged through.

As for essays and academic studies of his work, there is plentiful supply. A good selection of essays is *The Cambridge Companion to Beckett* edited by John Pilling (published by Cambridge University Press, 1996). *Samuel Beckett: Waiting for Godot/Endgame*, edited by

Peter Boxall (Icon Books, 2000), is a selection of interpretations on Beckett's two major plays. The *Faber Critical Guide to Samuel Beckett* by John Fletcher (Faber and Faber, 2000) is a precis of the life of Beckett and summary of *Godot, Endgame* and *Krapp's Last Tape*. All these books give a plentiful supply of different perspectives about Beckett.

Other references

It is also worth taking a cursory look through the biographies of actors and directors associated with Beckett. Books about modern art and music are worth looking at like Thames and Hudson's *New Media in the 20th Century* by Michael Rush (1999) and *Opera on the Beach* by Philip Glass (Faber and Faber, 1987) .

Beckett is an author who could pop up anywhere so keep your eyes peeled. Look at television comedy, theatre and literature. Look at comparative literature, obscure academia and modern, accessible culture. Beckett crops up in the most unlikely places as was (and is) his wont.

THEATRE PRODUCTIONS AND FESTIVALS

Throughout Europe and the Americas there is a constant supply of Beckett. Regular festivals take place in Germany and France and the odd revival in England takes place to celebrate the work of Beckett.

The Irish broadcaster, RTE, in association with Channel Four, are recording the complete theatrical work of Beckett for possible broadcast and educational work. He has always proven more popular abroad than he has in England but there always seems to be a Beckett piece in production somewhere.

ASSOCIATIONS, SOCIETIES AND STUDY

There are a number of associations and societies around the world devoted to Beckett. It is worth checking out the web site that is a treasure trove of links to Beckett devoted pages. It can be found at http://www.home.sprintmail.com/~lifeform/Beck_Links.html This will give you a huge amount of connections.

Reading University holds the Samuel Beckett Archive but you need permission to visit the place.

Reading University also runs a Master's Degree in Beckett studies. It is worth looking around other universities as Beckett Studies is becoming a popular area of research.

MODERN ART – PERFORMANCE ART, VIDEO ART AND INSTALLATIONS

The spectre of Beckett has wide tentacles. He lurks in the most unexpected places. It is worth keeping an eye open for art exhibitions of contemporary, electronic media. The galleries are starting to accommodate this kind of work and are prepared to present Beckett's work.

****SUMMARY****

- Go on a voyage of discovery.

- Do not limit yourself to theatre and books – go to the galleries as well.

- Keep an open mind – Beckett can be all things to all men.

- Try spotting Beckett in the world around you.

- No matter .

GLOSSARY

American Abstraction Art movement from America that explored the abstracted form of painting rather than a representation of a recognizable image.

Avant-garde Any artist, writer or musician etc. whose techniques or ideas are experimental and ahead of their time. Artists whose work is radical or daring for their time.

Dadaism An art group started in Germany at the end of the First World War. It reacted to the carnage of the war and the political landscape. It took an anarchistic approach which caused outrage.

Alighieri Dante 1265–1321, Italian poet whose most famous work is The Divine Comedies. The best known part is commonly referred to as Dante's Inferno.

Decentred universe A very anxious place where there are no fixed certainties, no absolutes. Everything is relative and so only definable in terms of something else which in itself lacks any degree of certainty.

Denouement The final clarification or resolution of a narrative.

Dramaturgy The study and practice of theatre and drama.

Experimental musicians A development of music gaining prominence in the 1940s onwards. The conventional forms of music-making, musical notation and musical performance were challenged and experimented with.

Feminism The study of gender politics from a female perspective.

Fluxus Literally meaning change. An international collective of artists, musicians, writers and film-makers that explored experimental art and the cross-fertilization between genres.

Futurists An art movement started in Italy in 1906 to celebrate the machine age and replacing traditional aesthetics.

Happenings Slang term for spontaneous artistic events, dating from the 1960s. It could be a performance of poetry or dance, protest, music, body painting etc. Anything that just happened.

Carl Gustav Jung 1875–1961 psychologist. Criticized Sigmund Freud's interpretations and developed analytical psychology. Developed the concept of the collective unconscious and its archetypes.

Metaphor A figure of speech in which a word or phrase is applied to an object or action that it does not literally denote in order to imply a resemblance.

Modernism Art movement of the late nineteenth and early twentieth centuries. The movement challenged established artistic conventions and celebrated new technologies and thought.

Naturalistic Art that is a true representation or copy of the world. The world is recreated on stage or in writing or paint.

Paradigm shift A movement away from the traditional or established rules. Relates to major, global change in thought or action.

Performance Art A form of artistic expression that uses live performance, installations, film and video. An artwork that is performed in a live or recorded form. Although culled from theatrical theory, its concerns are that of the artist as opposed to dramatist.

Pop Art Art movement started in America where the artist uses icons from popular culture to make their work.

Post-Modernism Art movement of the late twentieth century. Grew out of Modernism. Concentrated on *how* the artist sees rather than *what* the artist sees. The movement encouraged mixing genres, fragmenting forms and exploring the issues of nature, status and role.

Stream of consciousness Literary technique whereby a continuous flow of thoughts and feelings are expressed in long passages or soliloquies. A flow of recorded thought uninterrupted by conscious manipulation.

Structuralism In linguistics, any approach to the analysis of language that pays explicit attention to the way in which linguistic features can be described in terms of structures and systems.

Subliminal Information absorbed by someone without them being aware of the process.

The Surrealists A group of artists that moved away from Dada. Used notions of the sub-conscious to create their images.

Tableau A point of frozen time during or at the end of a drama. A static moment presented on stage.

Theatre of the Absurd A theatrical type whereby the normal conventions of theatre are ignored or modified to present life as irrational or meaningless.

Video art Any piece of artistic expression conceived for and recorded on video. Work shown in galleries either on television sets or by video projection onto a screen.

Zeitgeist The spirit, attitude or general outlook of a specific time or period.

Chronology of major works

1929	Publishes first essay '*Dante ... Bruno. Vico ...* Joyce in *Our Examination Round His Factification for Incamination of Work in Progress*' and first short story *Assumption*
1930	Composes the prize-winning poem *Whoroscope*
1931	Essay '*Proust*' published by Chatto and Windus
1932	Writes novel *Fair to Middling Women*
1934	The themed short-story collection *More Pricks than Kicks* published by Chatto and Windus
1935–36	Writes the novel *Murphy*. Published 1938 by Routledge
1941	Writes the novel *Watt*. Published 1953 by Olympia Press
1946	Writes the novel *Mercier and Camier* in French. Published 1970 by Les Editions de Minuit
1947	Writes the novels *Molloy* and *Malone Dies*. Published respectively 1951 and 1958 by Les Editions de Minuit
1948–49	Writes the play *Waiting for Godot* and the novel *The Unnamable*
1950	Writes *Texts for Nothing*
1953	*Waiting for Godot* first performed
1955–56	Writes plays *Endgame* and *Happy Days* for the stage and *All That Fall* for the radio
1958	Writes the play *Krapp's Last Tape*
1960	*How It Is* written
1961	Writes the plays *Happy Days* and *Cascando*
1963	Writes the play *Play* and the film *Film*
1964	*Film* is shot in New York with Buster Keaton
1965	Writes *Imagination Dead Imagine* and the television piece *Eh Joe*
1966	Writes *Texts for Nothing*. Films a version of *Play*
1972	Writes *Not I*
1974	Writes *That Time*
1975	Writes *Footfalls*
1980	Writes *Ill Seen Ill Said*
1981	Writes *Rockaby* and *Ohio Impromptu*
1982	Writes *Catastrophe*
1983	Writes *Worstward Ho*
1986–89	Writes *Stirrings Still*

INDEX